Arvin Vohra

HOW TO GET INTO AN IVY LEAGUE COLLEGE

2017

Published and distributed by
Roland Media Distribution
www.RMDGlobal.net

Edited by Chelsey M. Snyder

Cover Design by Ikmah Nahdi
Typesetting by Art Biro Network

ISBN: 978-0-9801446-9-7

HOW TO GET INTO AN IVY LEAGUE COLLEGE

ARVIN VOHRA

CONTENTS

INTRODUCTION 9

STRATEGIC OVERVIEW 15

THE TREATMENT EFFECT AND THE SELECTION EFFECT 15

PRISONER'S DILEMMAS AND INFINITELY REPEATED
GAMES 17

THE DIAMOND WATER PARADOX; THE PRINCIPLE OF
DIMINISHING RETURNS 20

DIMINISHING RETURNS 21

FINAL NOTE: THE TWO STEP ADMISSIONS 22

ACADEMICS 25

PRESENTATION 29

THE BASICS OF BECOMING AN ACADEMIC SUPERSTAR 32

STANDARDIZED TESTS 37

TWO INTENSE AND RUTHLESS STRATEGIES 49

RUBICON STRATEGY: LOCATION 49

RUBICON STRATEGY: RACE 53

EXTRACURRICULAR ACTIVITIES 59

THE ABSTRACT ART PRINCIPLE 62

THE CIGARETTE COMPANY PRINCIPLE 64

PICKING THE CENTRAL EXTRACURRICULAR ACTIVITY OF
YOUR APPLICATION 65

ENTREPRENEURSHIP 67

HOW MANY INTERESTING EXTRACURRICULARS SHOULD
YOU HAVE? 68

COUNSELOR QUESTIONNAIRES 73

CONTROL YOUR MESSAGE 74

THREE WORDS 79

STEAL PERSONALITIES LIKE AN EVIL SORCERESS 80

ESSAYS 87

   THE QUESTION OF BRILLIANCE 88

   OTHER WAYS TO START THINKING PROFOUNDLY 97

   UNIVERSITY ESSAYS 103

INTERVIEWS 113

   FIRST: DRESS 114

   ARRIVAL AND PREPARATION 117

   THE SMILE 119

   SHAKING HANDS 121

   EYE CONTACT 122

   POSTURE 122

   VOCAL CONTROL, VOCAL VARIETY 125

   NOW SEE AN EXAMPLE 129

   GESTURES 131

   WHAT TO TALK ABOUT 132

   CONTROLLING THE CONVERSATION: NON-SEQUITURS . . .133

   INTERESTING ANSWERS 135

HOSTILE INTERVIEWS. 137

MEMORABLE QUESTIONS 139

ADVANCED TECHNIQUES 142

FIRST GENERATION 149

ALTERNATIVES TO AMERICAN SCHOOLS 151

BRITISH COLLEGES. 151

SUPERIOR ALTERNATIVES TO ANY COLLEGE. 153

ABOUT ARVIN VOHRA. 163

INTRODUCTION

Many years ago, back in high school, I was academically exceptional. I had the highest grades in the hardest classes in my school, the highest PSAT and SAT scores in my graduating class, scores of 5 on ten different AP exams, and perfect scores on two SAT subject tests. I was the captain or president of several academic clubs, some of which I had founded or co-founded. I was a varsity athlete, and had done community service locally and abroad. I was a national merit finalist, an AP National Scholar, and had won many of my school's most prestigious awards.

When I applied to college, pretty much everyone thought I would get in everywhere. And yet, the exact opposite happened. I got rejected from one college after another, including some of my safety schools!

There was one spot of luck. Before I applied to Brown, I read an article someone wrote about the essay he used. I took his advice, and ended up getting into Brown. A tiny bit of luck at a critical moment opened that door.

But I want you to have more than just a tiny bit of luck. I want you to have an unstoppable strategy.

After my surprising admissions experience, I applied the same relentlessness that had made me an academic superstar towards learning about college strategy. I read tons of books and actual, successful college essays. I spoke to college admissions officers, and listened carefully to both what they said and what they did not say.

In 2001, I founded my own private educational company. From early on, college strategy was a major part of everything we did. I had learned the hard way that strategy was just as important as academics.

Today the college strategy division of Vohra Method is considered by many to have the most ruthless strategies anywhere. We do whatever is necessary to get the job done.

Unlike other services in our tier, we don't use bribery or large "donations" to ensure admissions.

Instead, we use subtle, devious strategies that make admissions officers want to admit our students. Admissions officers never know which students we work with. To the admissions officer, the students we help just seem like incredible diamonds they have discovered.

We are also very different from the lower tier programs, that focus on college matching. We don't waste time trying to see which city is the "best fit" for a particular student. Our students want to go to prestigious colleges. We get them there.

In this book, I'm going to teach you the strategies we use to set our students apart. It's not just about essay writing. An essay can get you pretty far, but a complete strategy can get you much farther.

You should plan to start your strategy by 7th or 8th grade. If you're already in high school, there are still plenty of things you can do, of course. But earlier is always better.

In fact, some of my most successful students started our programs as early as 4th grade! Obviously, the students don't think they are working on college strategy. They think they are just learning math or reading, but college strategy shapes even how we approach academics. I'll explain how in the academics section of this book.

Q: Wait, I thought college strategy starts in 11th grade?

A: Everyone on earth knows college strategy starts early, they just don't call it college strategy. They know they should try to get high grades, be in honors classes, join clubs, start playing sports, and/or play an instrument long before 11th grade. All that stuff is part of an effective college strategy.

No sane person would wait until 11th grade to start playing football, start playing a musical instrument, or take their first math class. Similarly, you shouldn't wait to do the additional strategies that are going to catapult your application above the rest.

STRATEGIC OVERVIEW

In order to understand college admissions strategy, you must understand the treatment and selection effects, the theory of infinitely repeated prisoner's dilemmas, the diamond-water paradox, and the principle of diminishing returns. Our approach to college strategy involves more abstract theory than those used by other firms. That's what gives us the advantage. Understanding this theory is the key to being able to create a world class college application.

THE TREATMENT EFFECT AND THE SELECTION EFFECT

In education, you have a "treatment" approach and a "selection" approach. A treatment approach means trying to make people smarter. A selection approach means trying to figure out which kid is already naturally the smartest.

Selection based education is mostly useless. It provides nothing to the student. It doesn't make him any smarter; it just tells other people how smart he already is.

Elite colleges rely almost entirely on the selection approach. In other words, they don't have particularly good training or education. Their classes aren't any better than those at community colleges. In fact, having personally attended both Ivy League classes and community college ones, I'd have to admit they are often a bit worse.

Instead, elite colleges choose the kids who are already mentally and academically superior.

Because of this, you need to convince colleges that you are a rare and magical diamond. **Not** that you just work hard. **Not** that you do the same extracurriculars as everyone else in a greater quantity. **Not** that you care more about grades. **Not** that you get more of your homework done.

You must convince colleges that there is something special and innate in you. And in order to do that, you will have to convince your school of the same thing, causing them to tell the college that there is something rare and amazing within you. So, to summarize:

Principle 1: Convince Colleges that you are Innately Rare and Special

PRISONER'S DILEMMAS AND INFINITELY REPEATED GAMES

If you study economics, you will study the prisoner's dilemma. Here's the situation:

Fred and Paul are involved in a robbery and get caught. If both maintain their silence, both get a month in jail. If both rat each other out, then both get 10 years in jail. If one person talks and the other is silent, the talker gets no jail time, but the silent person gets 20 years in jail.

The ideal situation: both keep silent. But that's not what game theory predicts.

Fred knows that no matter what, he should rat out Paul. If Paul talks, it's better to talk too. Then Fred will only get 10 years in jail instead of 20. If the Paul is silent, it's still better to talk because then Fred will get no jail time at all. Paul takes the exact same facts into consideration. The result: both talk, and both get 10 years in jail.

However, game theory gets more interesting if there is an infinitely repeated game. That means, two parties are locked in a repeating process. In our case, suppose Fred and Paul work together forever. Then, they could use strategies to make the other person keep silent. This would allow both prisoners to get lower punishments.

They may use a "tit-for-tat" strategy. Fred can tell Paul that whatever Paul does to him in round 1, Fred will do to Paul in round 2. Whatever Paul does to Fred, Fred does the same to Paul.

They may use a "trigger" strategy. Fred tells Paul: "I'll keep collaborating with you, as long as you keep collaborating with me. But if you tattle even once, I will never collaborate with you ever again."

So, how does all this relate to your college admissions?

Your school is locked into an infinitely repeated prisoner's dilemma with your desired college. Your school would benefit the most by having a student go to Harvard. It helps your school's reputation. They have a huge incentive to lie and say that some student is the greatest, smartest, most brilliant genius in history.

However, if your school lies to a college, or even stretches the truth, the college will retaliate. The college will stop trusting the school, stop accepting students from the school entirely, etc. If the college is nice, it might freeze your school out for a year or two. If not, it might freeze your school out permanently.

Colleges also have plenty to gain from working with your school. Your school has real, on the ground information about which students are truly extraordinary, and which just hired a journalism major to write them an essay. Colleges would strongly prefer to work with your school, rather than to break off the relationship.

So, with a general "trigger strategy" in play, the following truce has developed: colleges trust your school, and your school doesn't lie to colleges. A college believes pretty much anything your school says about you. After all, if your school lies, the consequences are disastrous for your school.

That means that if you convince your school that something is true, and it tells that to the college, the college will believe your school.

If your school thinks you are a rare, genetic genius, then it will tell that to the college. If your school thinks that you are one of your generation's visionaries, it will tell that to the college. And the college will, absolutely, 100% believe it.

On the other hand, if you tell the college that you are one of the major visionaries of your generation, they will just laugh at you.

Most amateur college strategists believe that college strategy is mostly about what you tell the college. They are wrong. Real college strategy is about what you tell your school. Real college strategy is about convincing your school that you are a rare and magical diamond.

Principle 2: Do college strategy to your school, not to the college.

THE DIAMOND WATER PARADOX; THE PRINCIPLE OF DIMINISHING RETURNS

Diamonds are expensive. Water is cheap. Water is necessary for life. Diamonds are necessary for nothing.

One reason that diamonds cost more is because they are rarer than water. Even though water is essential, it's common. It falls from the sky. Diamonds do not.

The same principle applies to college admissions. A college has accepted 999 people who are good at math and science, have high SAT scores, and high grades. Now there is one spot left. What will make a more interesting intellectual atmosphere: one more math nerd, or one kid who makes origami chess boards?

Of course, the college still needs people who are actually awesome at academics. If all 1000 students were making origami chess boards, but not good at math, you wouldn't have a college; you'd have a kindergarten.

The most effective strategy involves two parts. First, have excellent grades and SAT scores. We'll talk about how to make that happen in the Academics chapter. Second, have one or two things that make you radically stand out. To do that, you need to understand the concept of diminishing returns.

DIMINISHING RETURNS

Imagine the following situation: you are allowed to eat one ice cream sundae a year. One year, you are allowed to have a second one at the 6 month mark. How do you feel? Probably pretty excited (assuming you like ice cream sundaes).

Now let's say that you must eat one ice cream sundae every minute. Then, you are forced to eat an additional ice cream sundae in one minute. How do you feel? Probably nauseous.

The principle of diminishing returns basically says this: as you get more of a thing, each additional thing has less and less value. The 900th sundae is not as exciting as the first or second one.

Elite colleges see tens of thousands of nearly identical applications. They all look like this:

- High grades, sat scores, and AP scores
- Played piano or violin
- Internship at NIH or other large government research lab
- Community service at local nursing home or school, sometimes abroad.

All that stuff is good, but it's not rare. There is so much of it that college admissions officers are relieved to see pretty much anything else.

To stand out, you have to do something completely different (although you still need high grades and SAT scores, obviously.)

Principle 3: Be like a diamond, not like water. Be rare, not just essential.

FINAL NOTE: THE TWO STEP ADMISSIONS

Here's how the college admissions process works: first, a computer looks at your grades and SAT scores to make sure they are high enough. Second, if they are high enough, then a human reviews your essays, recommendations, and extracurriculars.

Note that a human will not bother with your grades and SAT scores. Uninformed students often tell each other that colleges care whether you take the SAT one time or three times. This is false. No one cares about minor details of your SAT scores.

As long as your SAT is high enough, you're fine. A 1600 SAT score is the same as a 1550 SAT score for college admissions. The only exception is for a recruited athlete, which I'll discuss later in this book.

Once your grades and SAT scores are high enough, don't obsess about minutia. Focus on big areas like essays, extracurriculars, and recommendations.

ACADEMICS

Academics are not enough to get you into an Ivy League college. But poor academics are enough to get you rejected. Fortunately, if you approach academics right, it will have great spillover benefits.

For example, let's say that you seem to be the smartest student in your math class. You seem to get concepts in seconds that others struggle with for hours. Your teacher then starts to think that you aren't just a hard worker, but a math genius.

What if you do that in 9th, 10th, 11th, and 12th grade? Now the whole school thinks you are a genius. What does your school tell colleges? What does your teacher tell colleges in her recommendation letter? What does your college counselor tell colleges in the questionnaire?

Will they tell colleges that you are just another hard worker? Or will they gush to colleges that you are the smartest genius that has ever attended your school?

Usually, they will gush and rave about how amazing you are. That's been the experience of many of my students. Their schools consider them genetic geniuses, chosen by god to be the leaders of their generation.

It obviously isn't true, by the way. My students succeed for the same reason anyone succeeds: hard work, perseverance, and intelligent techniques. Genetic ability has exactly zero to do with it. But it's fine to let others think something that helps you.

Here's what we do: in the summer before the school year starts, we have our students cover all the material for their conceptually hardest classes (math, science, philosophy, economics). For example, if they plan to take calculus in 11th grade, then we cover all of calculus in the summer after 10th grade!

By September of 11th grade, they know calculus. When their calculus teacher presents a new concept, they appear to understand it instantly, while everyone else struggles for 40 minutes. Obviously, they just struggled for 40 minutes during the summer. But the teacher doesn't see that struggle.

The key is that our students don't tell their teacher that they already did the work over the summer. They don't take a class for credit, or in their school's summer program, or any place that keeps official records. The teacher assumes that they are seeing the work for the first time.

School teachers, just like colleges, believe in the selection effect. They believe that their job is to help find which kids are genetically and magically the smartest. This belief is idiotic, but it is easy to manipulate. Because they are looking for innate genius rather than hard work, they see innate genius rather than hard work!

It is really easy to manipulate selection effect believers into believing that you are a rare and magical diamond. It pretty much requires 2 steps:

1. Get ahead academically. Learn the material beforehand.

2. Don't tell your teacher, school, friends, parent's friends, friend's parents, or even your own Siamese twin about it. Keep that training a secret, so they see magical genius, not hard work.

But this does mean that you must, absolutely, without question, be willing to do academic training outside of school that is not assigned by school.

Q: But no one in my class does it.

A: They probably do. They might be our students, who are carefully coached to never mention their outside of school training while in school. They might be one of the several million other people, who instinctively know the advantage of fooling their competition. They may understand that if they seem to be genetically super smart, you won't seriously try to compete with them. You'll think they are so far above you that it's not worth it.

But if no one in your class does it, that's even better news! That allows you to conquer them like conquistadors with steel armor and gunpowder facing American natives with stone arrowheads. It will be a blowout and a slaughter. That's what good strategy should look like! Good strategy doesn't mean winning by a few points. It means obliterating and completely demoralizing the competition.

You need to be willing to do what others are not. 1500 kids a year get into Harvard. A few million do not. Most of them don't even bother sending an application, since they know they have zero chance.

If you think or act like the average person, you have absolutely no chance. You must strategically outsmart the competition by acting radically different from how they act.

By the way, you'll probably end up doing less total work. If you learn on your own in the summer before, you'll try to learn in the easiest, simplest way possible. You'll watch Khan Academy or Crash Course videos, and read Barron's books. You won't assign yourself nonsense busywork. Then, when the teacher gives you silly assignments during the year, you will finish them in half the time. You learned the material efficiently, which allows you to defeat busywork quickly.

The really good news: in honors math classes, teachers usually put questions on tests that include topics you have not yet covered. That is there to make them a little harder. But if you learn the whole subject beforehand, you will often be the only one who can do those problems.

Imagine if your math teacher can say, "He got more challenge problems right than any other student I have ever taught" on the recommendation – and then use that to give credibility to the fact that you are a rising national expert on New Sports That Mimic the Lost Mayan Sports, or a creator of watermelon sculptures, or a designer of philosophical t-shirts? That's the key to getting in.

PRESENTATION

This also requires a very specific presentation. I'll illustrate with this story.

When I was in 9th grade, I loved biology. I'd gotten ahead in biology, and had the highest scores in the class on the biology SAT subject test.

However, I spent most of the year arrogantly mouthing off from the back of the class, arguing about grades, etc.

At the end of the year, one student gets a biology award. Not surprisingly, that student wasn't me. But despite my antics, I was given an honorable mention.

The next year, I decided to try things differently. I moved to the front, acted really interested. I didn't argue about test scores. I still got high grades, but I didn't act arrogant. Not only did I get the chemistry award at the end of the year, but the teacher coached me personally for the AP exam in chemistry.

Note that I actually liked biology more than chemistry. But a small change in behavior made a huge difference in result.

All the academic talent in the world won't help you if you act like an arrogant jerk, argue about grades, etc. You need to show the teacher that you are humble, down to earth, interested in the subject, and, most importantly, NOT motivated by grades.

Don't sit in the back of the class; sit in the front (unless you have assigned seating). Don't argue about test grades. If you get a point taken off unfairly, don't say, "Hey teacher! You owe me a point on this test." Instead, say, "I'm trying to figure out this problem I got wrong, but I'm having a lot of trouble understanding it. Can I meet with you to go over it?"

While you're "going over it", your teacher will notice the error, and adjust the grade. You look like you're focused on learning, not grades, and you still get the deserved points.

Never ask, "Will this be on the test." That just screams, "I don't care about knowledge or ideas. I just care about grades."

Instead, if you want to know if something will be on the test, just wait. Some other unstrategic moron will ask. He will damage his reputation; yours will be intact, and you will still know what will be on the test.

Your teacher must be convinced that your love of knowledge and ideas is so great that you cannot help but get the answers right. She must believe that you are not at all interested in grades. You must cultivate a persona of not caring about grades at all.

If someone asks you if you think grades matter, say, "No."

Never appear to put any thought into your grades at all. Don't hide your grades on tests. Don't display them either. Treat a grade the way you would a random smudge on a paper. Act as if it is the most insignificant part of anything.

That doesn't mean you actually stop caring about grades, as that would be idiotic. It just means you cultivate a persona of not caring about grades.

Most of what I've described here is most important in grades 7-12, but obviously more effective if you start early. In the next section, I'm going to explain what to do if you (or more likely your child) are younger than that. Ivy League admissions is serious business. The earlier you start, the better your chances.

THE BASICS OF BECOMING AN ACADEMIC SUPERSTAR

The key to being an academic superstar: do things versus your school, not with your school. Don't think of your teacher as your coach; think of him as the other team. Consider your school your opponent, not your ally.

That doesn't mean you need to disrespect your teacher. In fact, any competitor should respect his opponent. But that competitor should still know the difference between opponent and ally.

Recognize these two facts:

1. To get into an Ivy League college, you need to stand out. You need to set yourself apart from your competition at your school.

2. Your school is obligated to treat all students fairly.

Your school will not help you stand out from your peers, unless your mom or dad owns the school and isn't worried about appearing unfair. If you want to stand out, you're going to have to work around and against your school.

Your school will not help you get higher grades than your peers. It will not help you get higher SAT scores than your peers. It will not help you get higher AP scores than your peers. Your school will treat everyone equally.

But you don't want equality. You want victory.

Q: But every year, 20 people from my school go to Ivy League colleges, so it seems that they are doing a good job. Shouldn't I just put my faith in them?

A: Sure, 20 people get in, and 100 people don't. Unless your high school has a 90-100% Ivy Placement rate, I wouldn't put too much faith in their methods.

So, let's talk about how to achieve academic victory. I'm going to cover the academic techniques from the earliest ages. If you are a parent of a young child, you'll find the beginning parts relevant. But even if you are not, even if you are the parent of a high school student, or are yourself a high school student, read the early parts. Even if you are 16 now, you might be able to address some of the gaps in your own education, and improve your academic abilities more than you might have expected.

Note that this section assumes that kids attend school, and are not homeschooled. In other words, this section is designed to preempt the errors that schools will make, as well as take advantage of schools' vulnerabilities.

Of course, homeschooling can give a huge strategic advantage over regular schooling, but that is discussed later in this book.

Phase 1: Multiplication Tables

As American math teaching continues to deteriorate, no sane parent will rely on schools to teach math fundamentals. As of this writing, both public and private schools are using Common Core, which is the single stupidest curriculum I have ever seen. I'm sure in the future they'll find something even dumber. Here's what you need to do:

1. By age 5: Know addition tables.

2. By age 6: Know addition and subtraction tables.

3. By age 7: Know multiplication tables up to 10.

4. By age 8: Know multiplication tables up to 12.

Of these skills, the multiplication tables are by far the most important. They need to be absolutely memorized, not just "understood". Students must be able to instantly recall multiplication tables.

RIGHT:
Q: What's 7 times 8?
A: 56

WRONG:
Q: What's 7 times 8?
A: Ok, wait, I know this. Hold on. Ok, 7 times 7 is, I think, 49. So 7 times 8 is...fifty...fifty six!!

You have to drill these until they are automatic. If you like to use phone apps, you can consider Multiplication Synapse, an app that my company put together just to help kids memorize multiplication tables.

Q: But most kids aren't going to be able to do that.

A: True, most kids aren't academically in the top one percent. When you're applying to an Ivy League college, it helps to be, so you have to train hard. You need to be ahead of "most kids", not at the same level.

Parents who are not mathematically inclined may wonder why this is necessary. After all, don't kids just use calculators?

I discussed this issue extensively in *The Equation for Excellence*, but here's the gist: in order to do something like 1/a + 1/b, a student must be able to do questions like 1/3 + 2/7, and in order to do that quickly, you need to know your multiplication tables.

By age 9, the student must be able to do multi-digit multiplication and long division, using normal algorithms. Do not use lattice multiplication, long multiplication, or other inefficient idiocy.

By age 9, he should also be able to add fractions with unlike denominators.

Phase 2: Factoring

By age 12, the student should be able to quickly factor trinomials.

If some of these later topics are unfamiliar, you can hire basically any tutor to get the job done. You can also attend Kumon if you're on a very tight budget, or a Vohra Method math class if you want to really get ahead.

At this point, two things should have happened. First, the student should be dominating every math test. Second, he should be finishing his math homework really fast. With more time, the student should also gain a huge advantage in all other subjects, and be able to do much more with extra-curricular activities.

The second thing: the student should have learned to work independently of his school. Many kids are cripplingly psychologically dependent on schools. They literally cannot learn anything outside of school. Even when they do, they keep forgetting. While many elite tutoring services, including ours, have specific tools to change that, even for us it isn't easy.

Any student who can learn outside of school has a massive advantage over a student who cannot. The single most important academic skill your child should learn by age 12 is how to learn outside of school, without a teacher forcing him to learn.

STANDARDIZED TESTS

How do standardized tests fit into an overall strategy? Remember, the goal is to convince your teachers, administrators, friends, neighbors, local cashiers, and everyone else that you are a rare and magical diamond. You must convince them that you are innately special.

Standardized reasoning tests, such as the ERB,

ISEE, SSAT, Stanford Nines, Stanford-Binet IQ test, Weschler Tests, PSAT, SAT and others are a great way to do that. Most people view these tests as mysterious and incomprehensible. When someone does extremely well on one, they view that person with awe. This is exactly the result you're looking for.

Schools, particularly private schools, will often say, "We don't really look at these tests very seriously." They are lying. The fact is, those types of tests are frequently used to deny students access to honors classes.

Schools are just as much in awe of these tests as everyone else is. They don't really get how they work, and view these tests as a measure of innate ability. Doing well on such a test makes even your school feel a little awed.

So how do you do well on a standardized test? First, forget the idiotic notion that they measure something innate. IQ is 70 percent genetic, and 30 percent education and environment. An IQ of 100 is average, 130 is very high intelligence, and 70 is mentally retarded. In other words, 30 percent covers the range from the top to the bottom. Accept that you can prepare for any standardized test.

Then, learn how to directly solve the problems on the test. Work with a tutor, teacher, whoever. Don't waste time with people who focus on process of elimination. Find someone who teaches directly. If your budget allows it, consider Vohra Method. If not, find someone within your budget.

Do NOT take the school's advice and take it without studying. That is just following the diseased "selection effect" mindset, that pretends that ability is inborn instead of earned.

Q: What if I cannot easily find copies of the test I plan to take?

A: You can find sample tests on the website of the test or at Amazon. If it's something that is harder to get, like a Weschler test, try eBay. You can almost always get access to pretty much any test.

Parents: do not let your school know that you plan to study for the test! That defeats the entire strategy. Your school should not know that your child is studying for the standardized test. You should let your school know that you "don't believe in standardized tests", and then ask which tests they use. Enough people actually don't believe in standardized tests, so any school will believe you.

The same applies to students. Even if you are doing intensive SAT tutoring, DO NOT let your school know. If your school offers an SAT class on campus, don't take that one. Take any other SAT class anywhere. If your teacher asks, just say that you are more interested in <something rare and unique> than in standardized tests.

Your early standardized tests will set the stage for convincing your school that you are a rare and magical diamond. The critical tests happen in middle school and high school.

The PSAT

Your school will undoubtedly tell you that the PSAT doesn't count, that it's just practice for the SAT. Again, that's a lie. As a quick internet search will verify, a high PSAT score in your junior year is the ONLY way to become a National Merit Semifinalist. Being a semifinalist, in turn, opens the doors to many other scholarships and honors programs.

Your junior year PSAT is the most important standardized test you will ever take. You can take it only once, unlike the SAT or AP exams which you can take multiple times.

The practice PSAT tests you will take in your sophomore and freshman year are much less important. However, they are an opportunity to build your reputation as the rare and magical diamond.

You should start your PSAT training in 7th or 8th grade. If you are already past that age, and have not started, start today. Make sure you are working with a program that teaches direct solutions, not process of elimination and related nonsense. Ivy League admissions require world class scores, which come from serious training, not lazy and unreliable gimmicks.

AP Exams

If you remember the introduction, you'll recall that I got scores of 5 on ten different AP exams. Guess what: I didn't even take an AP class for six of them!

Most people know that you can technically take an AP exam without taking the AP course. But they think that only super smart geniuses can do that successfully.

The fact is that it's actually easier to get a 5 on an AP exam without taking the course at all!

Most AP courses are full of all kinds of extra busywork. For example, if you take AP biology, you have to do tedious labs, lab reports, make a model of a cell, dissect a shark, do an oral report about the heart, and god knows what else. All of that stuff takes a LOT of time.

On the other hand, if you just focus on the actual

academics, it's nowhere near that hard. If you study a Barron's book, memorize a spark chart, and watch some Khan Academy and Crash course videos, you courses have 3-5 times the actual information you need for the exam. This doesn't help; many students are so overwhelmed with this unnecessary information that they end up forgetting the information they actually need!

When you get a 5 without taking the test, people think you are a magical genius. It builds your reputation like nothing else can.

Not to brag too much more than I usually do, but I've done some intellectually impressive things in my life. I developed an individualized form of teaching that works in a group setting. I've developed an algorithm that makes memorization easier. I've developed a method of speed reading that actually works on complex texts. I've written several books.

No one, in my life, has ever found any of that as impressive as the fact that I took AP exams without taking the AP class. When you do that it will set you miles above anyone else.

You can do that with biology, chemistry, psychology, both English exams, and all the history exams. Yes, the exams are hard, but they are much, much easier than taking the course on top of studying for the exam. The course will just pile on extra work.

Of course, convincing your school is tricky. You don't want to seem all about the grades. Here's what I recommend.

Tell your school that you have been doing "independent research" in biology. Then, have your parents talk to the school, and let them know that you found some AP biology exams online and think you could actually do well on them.

Your school will push back. I promise you that. My school did. Every school that any of my students have ever attended also did. Your parents will have to fight. Let them be the bad guy. Your parents aren't trying to get recommendations from your school. You play the good, curious, intellectual. Let them be the achievement-focused elitists.

Train ridiculously hard for your first one.

If you decide to get tutoring or outside help, make sure you do it far away from your school. Your school must not find out. They must think that you are such a genius and innate intellectual that you just genetically got a 5 on the exam. Yes, I know it's an absurd belief, but most people believe that academic success comes from innate ability, not from hard work.

Take as many exams as you can manage. I've had

students graduate with as many as 16 AP exams, easily shattering my personal record. Like me, they took most of the exams without the associated course. Obviously, that actually made it easier for them, since they didn't have to do the school's busy-work. And it looks much more impressive.

The SAT Subject Tests

In addition to the SAT, you'll take some SAT subject tests. These are tests in biology, U.S. history, literature, etc. Each test is an hour long, and you can take up to three in a single day.

These tests are much easier than an AP exam. If you are already preparing for an AP exam, you should also take the SAT subject test in that topic.

The biggest mistake I see: people assume that their school course will prepare them for the SAT subject test. It almost never does.

AP courses at least try to prepare you for AP exams. Non-AP courses don't even try to prepare you for the SAT subject test. Your honors biology class will not prepare you for the SAT Biology subject test. Same for U.S. History, Chemistry, Physics, etc.

That's mostly because in non-AP classes, teachers tend to get a little distracted or political. Many biology teachers love to pontificate all day long about recycling and global warming, for example. Maybe that teaches some kind of civic responsibility, but it doesn't get you ready for the SAT Biology subject test.

You must train outside of school. I recommend using the Barron's SAT subject test book for the given topic. Don't waste time with the Princeton Review books; those are much easier than the real exam, and will only lull you into a false sense of security.

The SAT and the ACT

If you're reading a book like this, you probably already know you need to study for the SAT or ACT. You know that there is nothing sillier than studying for some minor quiz, and not studying for the SAT.

But how should you study? If you're trying to get into an Ivy League school, a middle of the road program like the Princeton Review or Kaplan is a waste of time. Learning how to do process of elimination and other gimmicks is not going to get you to an Ivy ready score.

You need to learn direct solutions. That means, you need to learn how to directly solve each math and verbal question without process of elimination, backsolve, or related nonsense.

There are programs for every budget. If all you can afford is a library book, I recommend using the Barron's SAT book. If your budget is under $700, consider a video based program, and get help from a local tutor. If your budget is 1000-2000, consider a Vohra Method program. If your budget is limitless, consider elite private tutoring.

When should you start training? My company recommends 7th-8th grade. Most of my serious competitors recommend...7th to 8th grade. We're all right.

Why not wait until 11th grade? Several reasons. First, your school will almost certainly not teach you what you need. You will have to learn it outside of school in one way or another. Second, you want to train before your 9th grade practice PSAT so you can start building a reputation.

Understand that serious SAT training is not a 6 or 8 week process. It takes at minimum several months; usually it takes a year, sometimes more. 6-8 weeks is just a placebo that allows your parents to avoid feeling guilty about not trying to educate you. It's not serious training.

Most people train for at least a year for an AP exam. The SAT is more important than any AP exam. Studying for only 6 weeks for an exam 50 times as important is just nonsense.

Multiple Attempts

Many students worry about taking the SAT or another standardized test "too many times." This concern is silly. That's not how college admissions works.

As mentioned earlier, college admissions has two steps. In the first part, a computer looks at your grades and SAT scores. In the second part, a human reads your essays and recommendations.

The computer does not care how many times you took a test. Why? Because you can do poorly on a test because of back luck, or bubbling wrong, or whatever. But you can't do well unless you actually know the material. Good scores tell the college information. Bad scores are inconclusive.

Take the SAT as often as you need to take it to get the score you want. The same applies to any other standardized test. Don't worry about "taking it too many times."

That said, don't just take it without doing any training. If you just keep taking it, you'll keep getting the same score. If you do serious training in between, you'll improve.

Taking a test 4-5 times is fine. But if you take it 30 times, you will start looking mentally ill.

Two Intense and Ruthless Strategies

RUBICON STRATEGY: LOCATION

One of the most famous moments in military history is Julius Caesar's crossing of the Rubicon. He crossed that sacred boundary and brought his army into Rome itself.

No Roman general had dared to do so before. It was such a deep and sacred rule that no one believed anyone would violate it.

There was no physical or military reason not to cross the Rubicon. There was just a very powerful psychological impediment.

In college strategy, there is a similar opportunity. There are things you can do, that will work, simply because no one would ever believe you would have the guts to do it. In my next book, I'm going to reveal the secrets on how to do it.

Just kidding. I'm going to reveal the secrets right now.

A little background: geographic location is a major consideration in college admissions. Colleges get too many applicants from New York, Boston, San Francisco, and DC. They get too few from Wyoming, Montana, Idaho, etc.

Ideally, every college wants to say that each class has students from all 50 states. However, even elite colleges can't. Most just settle for having someone from each state in each 4-year cohort. There will always be someone from Wyoming at the college, but not in each class.

Someone from Wyoming with a few AP scores and some powerful extracurriculars will absolutely get into the college of their choice. The problem: you don't live in Wyoming, or Idaho, or Montana...

...or do you? What if you could convince colleges that you are actually from Idaho?

Not everyone can do it. But if your parents work from home, own a business, travel a lot, etc., you can. Also, this system works primarily for those rich enough to not need any financial aid.

Here's how it works.

First, you establish residency in some unpopulated state like Idaho. Your parents register to vote there, you get your driver's license there, etc. They rent out some tiny cheap apartment as their official residence (not just a P.O. box).

You also make sure the state you pick has very relaxed homeschool laws, and register as a home-schooler.

You don't actually live in that state. You just take your SAT there, and your AP tests there. You can stay in any state for a couple weeks, it's no big deal.

You study independently, which you have to do anyway for any serious college strategy. You don't have to do the usual busywork, so you also have wayyyy more time for extracurriculars that put you out of the league of any competitors.

If you do all of this, your chances at an Ivy college are near 100%.

Q: If everyone starts using this technique, won't it negate the technique? In other words, if everyone from New York rents a cheap studio in Idaho and makes that their permanent resi-dence, won't this trick stop working?

A: I doubt that's a real concern. Very few people have even considered this technique. But even if every man woman and child on earth reads it, the technique will still work.

Only a tiny fraction of people will be able to do it. Most people don't have the employment flexibility to claim to work somewhere else. Only people who work from home or work online even have the option. Everyone else has a legal business address.

Of the people who can use the technique, very few will. Most people are very hesitant to use bold strategies (until they get rejected from their top choice college. Then, they usually get super angry, cry a bunch, blame each other, etc. Those who lack the courage to use the strategies that work also usually lack the courage to own up to the fact that they made a laughably weak decision, and have no one to blame but themselves.)

What if everyone starts working online and using these techniques? The most that will happen is that colleges will stop taking geographic location into consideration. That's great news if you live in a competitive state, but not if you live in an uncompetitive one.

By the way, homesteading is already used heavily by people seeking in-state tuition. Having legal residency in California, for example, gives you both lower tuition and admissions preferences for the University of California schools. Plenty of people just fake residency. There are all kinds of advisory services to help people do that, and not get caught.

It's much harder to pull off homesteading when you're dealing with in state tuition, since that's actually about money. If you're homesteading to make it easier to get into an Ivy League college, it's actually much easier.

Remember, Ivy League colleges know that being from Idaho, Montana, Wyoming, Alabama, or any of the other less competitive states doesn't give you an actual useful advantage. It just sounds cooler if they can say, "We have students from 50 states and 90 countries" rather than "We have students from 47 states and 90 countries." In other words, they don't want to out you. If you're convincing enough, they can say they have 50 states. It isn't to their advantage to look too deeply, since if they do, they will have to swap a fake resident with great credentials and ability for a genuine resident without them.

They aren't losing any actual money. If this was about tuition, sure, they'd crack down as much as they could. But even with those crackdowns, as happens with in-state tuition, you can still do homesteading. In this case, there is no money to be lost, making it even easier.

RUBICON STRATEGY: RACE

Race plays a major role in college admissions. If you are Hispanic, Native American, or Black, you have a major advantage.

But you can't just say, "Hey! I'm Black!" and expect that to accomplish anything. You have to show that your ethnicity contributes to the diversity on campus. You need to show how being Black shapes the way in which you study and perceive physics, or history, or something. You need to show how your Native American heritage shapes how you interact with gender, or math, or your own internal self.

But what if you aren't in one of the underrepresented categories? Don't despair.

A famous successful Harvard essay is written by an African American woman who looks white (her mom is white). She talks about how different it was being someone who appears white but is actually black. It's a compelling and unusual story.

You know who else could write that story? Literally any white person ever. Many elite colleges don't bother to verify SAT scores. You think they'll check your mom or dad's race? Just set up some photoshopped pictures on facebook, set your profile to public. If the admissions officer is curious, that's where they'll look.

Actress Mindy Kahling's brother pretended to be black to get into medical school. And it worked.

In fact, Rachel Dolezal, a white woman, used a little hair and makeup adjustment to become the head of the Spokane NAACP!

If you go to a small private school that actually knows the parents, this obviously won't work as easily.

But if your dad has brown hair, couldn't he be half Cuban? Or entirely Cuban, but your great grandfather had to change his last name when they immigrated?

If you're East Asian, isn't it hard being biracial <wink>, and facing discrimination from your own family?

If you're going to pull a con like that, by the way, you need to start very, very early.

The second most ruthless college strategist in the country (after yours truly), is East Asian. East Asians are "overrepresented" minorities in colleges, so it is harder for East Asians to get into elite colleges. You know what he did before his first child was born? Changed his last name to something obviously not Asian.

You might not feel comfortable with such an aggressive race strategy. No problem. You have some kind of race. Maybe you're part English. Maybe you're Japanese. If you can discuss, in your application essay, how that cultural ancestry shapes some part of the way in which you intellectually interact with the world, then you are officially someone who contributes to campus diversity! It's hard to do, but plenty of my students have managed to do it pretty effectively.

The key thing: don't make it a cliché. Find something completely unusual, even if it's mostly made up, that will help you stand out.

WRONG: From my Indian parents, I learned the importance of hard work and education. (This sounds cliché, tedious, boring, and obvious).

RIGHT: Hindu culture considers the material and spiritual world to be commingled. The material world is considered an extension of thought, not just mundane matter. When I began to study non-Euclidean geometry, my grandfather's many discussions on this topic finally made sense. (This sounds awesome.)

EXTRACURRICULAR ACTIVITIES

Most of my students spend thousands of hours on very difficult extracurricular activities. Some become elite pianists, others spend years doing research at NIH or a similar government lab. But when it comes time to write the application, all that work is not very useful.

In fact, we often either downplay or don't even mention those laborious activities!

In other words: the thousands of hours spent on all that stuff was basically a waste of time. All those piano lessons, all that time being miserable in a lab, all that time volunteering in a nursing home: totally pointless. They do absolutely nothing for an Ivy League application.

As we discussed in the diminishing returns principle, a successful Ivy League application stands out. It doesn't just do the same exact stuff as every other applicant. It doesn't do slightly more stuff than other applicants. The fact that you play piano at level 11, but others play it at level 10, does not matter at all. The fact that you took 16 AP exams and other people took only 4, also doesn't matter enough.

Standing out means completely, totally standing out. I'm going to give some real examples. Most of these are not even my students, but either people that I met or learned about through admissions officers:

1. One person had a small business where she made and sold origami earrings. Whether the business was successful, or sold more than a single pair, is irrelevant.

2. One person made an independent blog, website, and YouTube channel about a particular branch of philosophy.

3. One person worked on several projects related to making minimalist items, and launched a couple Kickstarter projects related to that. These were not projects that raised millions, but raised probably a pretty small amount of money.

4. One person created a soft drink company (in reality, mostly just created a website for a soft drink company).

5. One person ran social media for a few local political candidates.

Note that none of these took nearly as much time as standard extracurricular activities. These people didn't have to work as hard as all-state musicians, or all county athletes. They didn't have to put in hundreds of hours, the way many who focus on community service do.

They were all essentially in a category that contained one person. There was no competition, so they didn't have to work overly hard. They just had to do anything at all, and they stood out.

Those that started early (before 9th grade) were often featured in school newspapers or local newspapers. But even those that started late still got into top tier, elite colleges.

When picking an activity, ask yourself this: Is anyone else you've ever heard of doing this activity? If the answer is yes, do something different.

Are there 100 people in the Young Republicans club in your school? If so, pick something else.

Does your school's entrepreneurial club have 40 people? Pick something else.

Do many people in your area do an internship at NIH? Do something else.

Do soooo many of your friends recommend CTY because they enjoyed it soooo much? Do something else. Doing what others do will not help you stand out.

Does everyone in your area go compete in a particular debate league? Pick something else.

THE ABSTRACT ART PRINCIPLE

Pretty much no one can tell if a particular abstract art painting is good or bad. Even collectors have a hard time figuring it out. Articles have been written that show the huge auction price differences between nearly identical abstract paintings.

So how do most of us actually judge abstract art? We look at the surroundings. If we see an abstract art painting in the Museum of Modern Art, we assume it's pretty good. If we see an identical painting in a stoner's basement, we assume it's less good.

Colleges work the same way. If you say you made a comic strip on the inside of a watermelon, they don't know if that's good or bad. So they will look at the surroundings.

On your college application, you will be able to list 5-10 extracurricular activities. If they all look like "watermelon comic", you may just look unhinged. Instead, you put in a mix of things that they can understand (e.g. Model U.N. president) and weird things (e.g. Egyptian Poet). The normal things provide a sense of legitimacy to the weird things.

Suppose you were the class president and also made cell phone cases that represent various historical wars, like the Punic Wars. Which do you put first?

Most people would erroneously put the class president first. They may think it's more impressive, takes more effort, etc. They may think, "These cell phone cases took like 20 minutes on CafePress, while being class president took a ton of effort."

But that's totally wrong. Here's the fact: the college doesn't know how good the cell phone case thing is. So, they are waiting for you to tell them.

Fortunately, they do know how good class president is. Maybe they think it's 20 units of good. If you put class president above cell phone cases, then they will assume your cell phone case thing is 19 units or less of good.

If you put cell phone cases above class president, they will assume that the cell phone cases are 21 or more units of good!

You should make the top thing on the list something unusual, and the second thing something known. You can also make the top two things unusual, and the third thing known.

But don't push it farther than that. If you have more weird things, put them after the known thing.

Note: weird just means unknown. So, if you win a major film festival, that counts as known, not as something weird. Weird means not having any standard measurement option. So, if something is in any way official, it is not in the weird category.

If you win an award for a thing, then it can count as known. If your school endorses a thing in some official way, it also counts as known.

THE CIGARETTE COMPANY PRINCIPLE

People often point out that cigarette companies and other socially hated companies will often donate a small amount to a charity, and then spend millions telling everyone that they donated to that charity.

You must do something similar to get the best result. Suppose you decide to make a blog about ancient Egyptian poetry. Here are the steps:

1. Make a blog and website about ancient Egyptian poetry. As of this writing, I recommend Squarespace.

2. Do a few YouTube videos about stuff you've learned.

3. Most important: tell your teachers, and have your parents tell your teachers as well. Get some Egyptian style jewelry for $2 on Amazon, so that everyone knows that's what you're about.

4. If your school has assemblies or school meetings, ask your school if you can do a presentation there.

5. Write your local newspaper, or ask to put an article in your school newspaper about this issue.

The total time for something like this is around 40-200 hours. Doing 200 hours of community service, or lab research, or piano practice will accomplish basically nothing. Doing 200 hours of something random will guarantee your admissions (assuming you have high enough grades and SAT scores).

The college will have about 9 billion people who played piano, and another 9 billion who did community service, and 10 billion who did lab research. If you are the only one who has expertise in Egyptian poetry, you will stand out like a rare and magical diamond in a pile of coal.

PICKING THE CENTRAL EXTRACURRICULAR ACTIVITY OF YOUR APPLICATION

How do you come up with something unusual enough?

First, don't ask your parents. Parents: don't ask yourselves. Parents are always wayyyyy too conservative to think properly outside the box.

In the many years I have worked with students, I have had many students come up with great ideas.

I have had zero parents manage to. Here's what it's like:

Student Idea: Maybe I can make a series of web comics that talks about the history of garbage cans.

Parent Idea: Maybe you can talk about how you play the piano...wait for it....at a nursing home!

Note to kids: Having kids is often terrifying. Parents are afraid of making mistakes. That's why so many parents just copy other parents. Better to take the safe path than to mess things up.

Teenagers, on the other hand, generally consider themselves immortal, and take huge risks for no reason. That's the type of thinking you need in this case.

When picking whatever you want to work on, start with your actual interests. Not your favorite class in school – you only take 6 classes, so 1/6 of the people in your school probably like that same subject. I mean something totally unique to you. Something that you like, that others don't like. It can be artistic, political, entrepreneurial, historical, whatever. Think of the things you liked as a kid, or are fascinated by now. It's different for every person.

If it's piano, violin, or science research, that's the wrong answer, obviously. If it's Aramaic, water guns, candy sculptures, monetary history, musical language, now you're getting close.

In general, I've found that entrepreneurship, authorship, fine arts, and politics are the most effective areas, but certainly not the only areas that work. Let's go over some examples on how to use each of those.

ENTREPRENEURSHIP

Some types of entrepreneurship focus on a single area. For example, if you are interested in chewing gum, entrepreneurship might involve making a brand of chewing gum with some unusual features. If you really like comic books, entrepreneurship might involve making a comic book, creating a website that reviews comic books, etc. If you really like music, entrepreneurship might involve creating a business that sells music accessories, or a music review site, or even writing songs or jingles.

Many of the most effective types of extracurricular entrepreneurship involve interestingly combining two areas. For example, let's say you like Japanese history and candy. A candy that explores this history of Japan (maybe on the inside of the wrappers), or a website+blog+youtube channel that looks at the history of Japanese candy would stand out way more.

HOW MANY INTERESTING EXTRACURRICULARS SHOULD YOU HAVE?

I would say 1-3 highly unusual extracurriculars is ideal. I have also seen successful applications with as many as 5.

But don't dilute the message. Don't put 2 good ones, and a third that falls flat. Look at the following two lists:

List 1:

1. Founder of Shoeplant, which uses plants to make woven shoes for orphans.

2. Winner, Maryland Minority Film Festival, Short Animated Documentary Category.

List 2:

1. Founder of Shoeplant, which uses plants to make woven shoes for orphans.

2. Winner, Maryland Minority Film Festival, Short Animated Documentary Category.

3. Member, English Club

List 2 looks much weaker than list 1. The presence of the flat, uninteresting, common activity, done at a low level (the person is a member, not an officer) just makes the rest look like a façade, a lie, or a joke. It brings down the other activities. Realistically, even if the person were an officer here, it would still be better to exclude that particular item.

Now let's fix list 2.

List 3:

1. Founder of Shoeplant, which uses plants to make woven shoes for orphans.

2. Winner, Maryland Minority Film Festival, Short Animated Documentary Category.

3. Working on a novel about Cambodian refugees called "Red Sunset of the Khmer."

Now it looks like it means business. "Working on a novel" means literally nothing, but it sounds awesome. List 3 shows a person who is about doing big, exciting things. List 2 is just someone trying to fill up a resume.

By the way, it may seem like item 2 is too high. Shouldn't winning a film festival go lower down, so it can push the other things up?

Not really. First, a Maryland Minority Film festival doesn't really exist, and if it did, it wouldn't have more than maybe 2 entrees in the Short Animated Documentary Category.

But even if you won at Sundance or Cannes, the

two most influential film festivals in the world, I would recommend putting that pretty high. Here's the difference.

Winning a film festival, while measurable, is extremely unusual and interesting. Thus, you want to highlight it. It should be an emphasized feature for your application, not just something to add legitimacy.

Things like "NIH Internship" or "Class President" are not unusual or interesting, and should only be used to add legitimacy, since thousands of people do research internships, and every single school in the country has a class president. Winning something artistic or scientific (e.g. a major science fair) should be an emphasized showpiece.

A list of five items might be:

1. Founder of Shoeplant, which uses plants to make woven shoes for kids who live in high heat environments.

2. Winner, Maryland Minority Film Festival, Short Animated Documentary Category.

3. Working on a novel about Cambodian refugees called "Red Sunset of the Khmer."

4. NIH Genetics Research Internship exploring a possible cure for the A1C3M5 genetic anomaly.

5. Captain, Varsity Golf Team

Now that's a list! It looks impressive, flashy, and has things to add legitimacy. The person looks strong, creative, innovative, respected in the community, worshipped by fans, working to save humanity, blah, blah, blah. Here's what that list actually means:

1. I made a website

2. I won by entering a small competition with very few contestants.

3. Nothing at all

4. Lab drone who did sub-entry-level work

5. The only golf player in your school

The point here isn't that you aren't exciting, or can't be. The point is that you just don't need to do all that much work to get the job done. Decide what you're about, do a little work, brag about it a lot (like the cigarette companies), and get into the college of your dreams.

COUNSELOR QUESTIONNAIRES

As I mentioned earlier, colleges trust your school – but they don't trust you. Your school will be working with the college admissions office forever. You, on the other hand, will have a single interaction with that admissions office. You have every incentive to lie, so colleges just don't trust you as much.

But here's the good news. Your college counselling office will give you a questionnaire. They will use that questionnaire to write your official recommendation from your school. Anything in that recommendation will be completely believed by every college.

The good news: your college counsellor will basically copy and paste your questionnaire answers onto the official recommendation.

Think about the opportunity that gives you. The college won't believe you. But they will believe your counsellor. And your counsellor will tell the college anything you want him to.

If you tell the college you are really interested in extinct butterflies, they will assume you are lying.

If you tell the counsellor that you are really into studying extinct butterflies, he will then tell that to the college, and they will 100% believe it.

The even better news: almost every student totally blows off the college counsellor questionnaire. They think, "I'm applying to college, not to my college counsellor. Who cares what he thinks?" They don't know the magic of the college counsellor questionnaire.

That means that when you put quality answers, your questionnaire automatically stands out above your competitors'.

Now let's talk about what to actually put on your college counsellor questionnaire. If you've gotten the ideas of this book so far, you've probably figured it out.

You should focus the entire questionnaire on 1-3 unusual, interesting things. Remember, your job is to stand out.

CONTROL YOUR MESSAGE

Imagine if the president gave the following speech:

"Today, I'm proud to announce the economy is

better than it has been in the last century. New construction is up. The employment rate is at record highs. Every industry – IT, automotive, medicine, even butterfly raising – is doing well. Speaking of butterflies, sometimes I wish I were a butterfly. We are de-escalating every armed conflict and bringing our troops home."

What would the press pick up on in this good news speech? My guess: "Sometimes I wish I were a butterfly." Within 12 hours, he'd be known as President Butterfly.

Controlling the message is vital in politics. It's even more vital in college applications.

Suppose you have your entire college counsellor questionnaire focusing on a business that sells feathers to raise awareness about hippos. However, in one part you mention that you play violin, and in another part you mention your NIH internship. Guess what part makes it to your official recommendation? Yup. The NIH internship and the violin. Now you're just another, run of the mill, boring nerd. Your unique application is completely ruined.

Plus, when colleges read about the feather hippo project on your application, it looks like you're lying.

Note that your college counsellor was just trying to help. Unlike the author of this book, your college counsellor is probably a pretty decent, kind person, not a ruthless sociopath. He sees the college admissions process as a reasonably fair, straightforward process. He doesn't think it requires mind games and manipulation. So, he's giving the college the kind of down to earth, pragmatic information he thinks they would value.

Chances are, his definition of "success" is much lower than yours. He thinks success means getting into a decent, respectable college. You want to get into Harvard.

His techniques are a knife in a gun fight. Our techniques are bringing a tactical nuke to a game of Candyland.

And the vast, vast majority of college counsellors are not modern Ivy League graduates from competitive groups. Some are very old, and got into an Ivy League college back when only 2 percent of the population went to college. Others applied from rural Idaho, or came from underrepresented minority groups that have a much, much easier time getting in to competitive colleges.

Some counsellors, however, are relatively recent Ivy League grads, and not from any privileged group (i.e. they are not underrepresented minorities, and not from an undesirable state). Those counsellors will pretty much always give strategic advice similar to ours.

Long story short, you need to control your message. You need to make sure that every single sentence in your questionnaire leads to the interesting activities that are the focal point of your essay. Here are some examples.

QUESTION: What are your favorite classes?

WRONG ANSWER: I really liked chemistry because it was challenging.

RIGHT ANSWER: I loved how I could use what I learned in chemistry to help in my watermelon comic project. In this project, I used some of the acids and oxidizers we learned about in chemistry, and applied them to watermelon comics. I discussed these reagents with my teacher, and even based a watermelon comic scene on it.

Note that every single sentence mentions watermelon comics. No matter what the counsellor choses to copy/paste, he's going to mention the watermelon comic.

QUESTION: Which teachers have you liked the most?

WRONG ANSWER: I really liked Mr. Francis because he challenged me and was patient.

RIGHT ANSWER: I really liked the way Mr. Francis discussed practical applications of history, which I later used in my cell phone case war history project.

Mr. Francis made history come alive and feel relevant, and I was inspired to try to do the same through the cell phone case war history project.

Got it?

In 2016, I was the Vice Chair of the Libertarian Party. In pretty much every interview, I constantly talked about dramatically cutting government, which is the primary goal of the Libertarian Party. Most journalists prefer softer messaging, and try to water down the message. With me, however, this is pretty hard since I make sure each sentence is hard-hitting.

One TV station finally managed to outsmart me. They interviewed me for about 30 minutes straight for a pre-recorded interview, from which they would take about 30 seconds of footage. Understanding this, I made sure each sentence was about majorly cutting government. The TV station used HALF of a sentence from my interview in which I was talking about something else (the other half of the sentence talked about cutting government)! They couldn't get a full sentence, so they went with half a sentence.

I want you to keep that in mind when you are doing your questionnaire. Make sure that every single sentence is on point. Your college counsellor probably won't quote only half a sentence from the entire questionnaire, but he might quote only one sentence. It'll probably be the sentence in which you mention that you have a sibling and play the piano, like every other nerd on earth.

THREE WORDS

One common question that students mess up: "Come up with 3 words to describe yourself".

First, don't choose "creative, hardworking, intelligent, ambitious, persistent." Your goal is to stand out, not to give the same answers as everyone else. Second, those words are prerequisites for applying to an Ivy League college. If you aren't intelligent and hardworking, you aren't even a candidate.

Saying, "I'm intelligent and hardworking" would be like a Mercedes ad that said, "The new Mercedes S class has four wheels." That's good to know, but not a reason to buy an expensive car.

Understand this: the market price of a Harvard degree is around 1.5 million dollars. The actual tuition is about $200,000 as of this writing. That means that when Harvard admits a student, they are investing about $1.3 million worth of brand equity into that student. That student better be a hell of a lot more than just intelligent and hardworking.

So what words should you use? Consider the personality differences between yourself and your best friend. Try to describe those.

(NOTE: If your best friend is not intelligent and hardworking, get new friends. Lazy and stupid people are anchors that will drag you down, not friends who will make you better.)

Here are some examples: subtle, brazen, outspoken, inconspicuous, excitable, ice-calm, lyrical, laconic, talkative, observant, dreamer, etc.

But you don't just list the word! You tie it to the centerpiece of your application. For example:

"Laconic – I like to find nonverbal ways to communicate, which is one reason that I started creating a language based on dog hair instead of words."

"Observant – In fact, I noticed an interesting shape in a discarded watermelon rind, which is how I started making watermelon comics."

Don't do this:

"Stupid and fearful – which is why I'm going to talk about the same NIH internship and piano lessons all my competitors do. Better to play it safe than to actually succeed!"

STEAL PERSONALITIES LIKE AN EVIL SORCERESS

One of the more advanced techniques we use at Vohra Method is called stealing personalities.

The fact is, you're like me. You want to get into an Ivy League college for personal gain. You want to be more financially, intellectually, or creatively effective. You want college to give you advantages. If you're not "privileged", you want to become privileged. If you are privileged, you want to become more privileged. If you're in the top 10 percent, you want to move up to the top 1 percent. If you're already there, you want to move to the top 0.000001 percent.

You don't care about social justice, or being nice, or any of that, at all. (Note: if you do, then this process is even easier!) You want to get into the most prestigious college so you can get more out of life.

Here's the problem with that: the college admissions process is designed to screen out people like that. They don't want a bunch of narcissistic, selfish, sociopaths. They want the opposite. So, what do you do?

I like to use a technique called "stealing personalities." Here's how it works. When I meet people who are all about social positivity, or more interested in research than personal gain, or whatever, then I immediately start to get to know them. I ask all kinds of questions to learn about their motivations, family, childhood experiences, etc. They are different from mine and yours in important, but subtle ways. Learning those subtle cues will help you seem like the type of person colleges want.

It's actually a lot like espionage! Russian spies have to learn to seem like normal Americans, and American spies need to learn to seem like normal Russians. You need to learn to seem like a social justice academic, rather than an awesome, selfish, badass.

Graduate students, professors, social justice advocates, and nonprofit workers are great for this. I like to ask them why they picked their graduate program, what they want to do with their research, what changes they want to make in the world, what they're working on right now, etc. Despite my own elitism, most social justice people consider me a great listener, since I am literally memorizing every word. I've often spoken to people working in these areas for hours, learning their life stories, so that we can use them later on.

Some of our most basic techniques we use at Vohra came from these discussions. For example, colleges often ask, "Why do you want to go to this college?" People like me and you find that question bewildering. We want to go to that college because it's prestigious, has good academics, and will give us personal advantages. Instinctively, we know not to actually say that, but then we're left wondering what else to say.

Social justice nerds have helped us answer this question. When you ask them why they picked a particular graduate program, they often will discuss the specific research of a specific professor. Today, most Vohra students do the same in their application. Obviously, they are faking it, but they know what to fake. While other people make pointless lies about how many community service hours they did, we make sure that our clients tell the right lies.

I've talked to scientists about what fascinates them about science, peace advocates about what their current challenges are, etc. I ask them especially about their childhood experiences. Many of our students borrow those childhood experiences for their own essays.

Consider how convincing it is to the admissions officer. You see an applicant whose childhood experiences, method of choosing a school, and current desires exactly match the type of applicant you're looking for. It looks real, not like the usual laughable attempts that high school students use to lie. It's just too convincing to be a fake.

Creating such a counterfeit personality for your application should be started early. Make sure you put that same information on your college counselor questionnaire. Make sure your parents put that same information on their college counselor questionnaire. For example, if you want to copy someone's story about how they got interested in chemistry, make sure that that story appears on your college counselor questionnaire! Don't worry, no one will suspect a lie. People don't usually have the intelligence to lie about something like that. Most people just inflate their number of community service hours, or make up some silly excuse for a low grade.

Interestingly, when you go through the process of stealing personalities, you often make really interesting friends. You quickly move past small talk and into more interesting conversations. I've made many friends in this process who consider it a high and hilarious compliment that their personalities are used as a basis for so many applications. They realize that imitation is the highest and funniest form of flattery. (NOTE: I don't tell them this until after I know them, and have verified that they find my general amorality funny, not terrifying.)

If you're really shy, two things: First, work on that. I was pretty shy as a kid. Getting over that was the smartest decision I ever made. Yeah, it takes a bunch of work. It's worth it.

Second, you can get the same result by attending lectures by literary authors or scientists. They will often talk about their motivations for what school they attended, their early experiences, etc. If they don't, just ask them in the Q&A session. If you're too shy, have a friend or parent ask the question for you.

Don't mimic their answers exactly. Just get a sense of their motivation.

ESSAYS

People do the same things with college essays:

1. Dread them.

2. Get really afraid and nervous.

3. Write fearfully.

4. End up writing the same boring essay as everyone else.

It's no surprise. It's a high pressure essay, and most students have not been trained to write like that. Colleges are looking for a professional level personal narrative. (Note: many people make their livings writing personal narratives for magazines.) You haven't learned to write a professional personal narrative. Most schools only teach you to write amateur level literary analysis, even though only maybe 3 people in human history have made a living writing literary analysis.

Your college essay needs to be 1. Personal, and 2. Brilliant.

Brilliant is harder, so we're going to start with that.

THE QUESTION OF BRILLIANCE

First, what does brilliance mean in a college essay? It means that at some point in the essay, the reader stops and says, "Wow. I would never have thought of it that way."

It doesn't need to be every sentence. It doesn't need to be at the beginning. Just somewhere, in at least one place, the reader needs to say, "I would never have thought of it that way."

At first, that seems like an impossible request. But there is a trick to this.

"Brilliance" often comes from finding:

1. Similarities between very different things.

   OR

2. Differences between very similar things.

This process lets you discover an interesting idea to talk about. You might never mention the specific things you started out with; you will probably just use the ideas that this process leads you to.

We will use this process to create a key sentence

or paragraph somewhere in the essay.

The overall process will look like this:

1. Pick two things that are totally different.

2. List a lot of similarities. Then, find the ones that are interesting and not at all obvious.

3. Those will be used to create a theme

4. Then, you will write an essay with that theme.

We'll start with this essay, taken from *Lies, Damned Lies, and College Admissions*.

In this example, the student begins with Latin and Golf. These are two totally different extracurricular activities. Then, we find similarities between them. Then, we use the non-obvious similarities to create a cool theme.

You make a list of similarities:

1) Both are hard and require patience

2) Both happen in school

3) Golf was invented in Scotland, where Latin had some influence on the language.

4) In Latin, word order does not matter. For example, the verb can be in the beginning, middle, or end of a sentence. Similarly, golf is nonlinear. You are seeking a goal, but it's not a simple forward backwards like soccer or football.

5) Both are "useless." Latin has no direct application, and hitting a ball into a hole is objectively
pointless.

6) Both force you to strive for excellence for its own
sake. Latin is not a means to communication,
since no one speaks it. The study of Latin is an
end in itself. Golf does not make you stronger. It
is also an end in itself.

7) Etc.

Now we use only the points that are actually
interesting. Items 1-3 are totally boring, so we skip
them. Here are a few examples of how you might
start an essay:

You might start with a crazy statement, like "I
love useless activities."

You could start with some vivid part of a story,
like "My eyes trace the Latin inscription at the base
of the weathered marble pillar. 'Nature, Community, Strength.'"

Or some third thing.

Now, I'm going to pick one of those ideas as a
theme. Looking at item 4, I pick "nonlinear" as a
major focus. Obviously, I need to add some kind of
childhood made up story about nonlinearity. Here
is an example essay:

When I was in first and second grade, my father and I used to play an unusual game. We would make up a story together, but instead of writing it down on a sheet of paper, we would write the individual sentences on separate note cards. When the story was finished, we would shuffle the note cards and see what new tales emerged.

The new characters illustrated unexpectedly brazen responses to traditional situations, ("The witch threw Fred into the oven. 'I hope I get a bicycle for my birthday,' said Fred."), and novel scenarios ("The witch threw Fred into the oven. He saw a dark staircase, covered with mud.").

When I got a bit older, I did the same with comic strips in the newspaper. At first, I would just rearrange the squares of a single strip, but things became much more interesting when Family Circus, Spiderman, and the Piranha Club merged into one narrative.

And in a bizarre way, it became more honest. My father, an engineer and an artist, has a saying that he says at least 10 times a week: "Hell is other people." Beneath the joke is my father's fundamental view that when you work on your own projects, you can pursue private excellence. But as soon as you get involved with other people's problems, things get messed up. Your visions, your plans, necessarily get diluted and corrupted.

My bizarre juxtaposition of images of unrelated comics were part of my first inkling that I fundamentally disagreed with that view. What would be the point of Spiderman's battle with Dr. Octopus if the other characters in the other strips didn't exist? Why invent a car if there is no one to drive it?

My nonlinear comic strip narratives became a fundamentally different way of looking at the world. As crazy as the nonlinear comics were, the real world was more so. I prepare for a chemistry test. Then a couple is beaten to death in Afghanistan for not following the religious requirements. Then someone eats a sandwich. Then Google leaves China. Then someone turns a page in Hamlet. Then a child searches through garbage for food.

In Latin, unlike in English, word order within a sentence doesn't matter. If you rearrange all the words in a Latin sentence, you get the same meaning. To me, that part of the language is beautiful, frustrating, and a perfect analogy for how I look at the human world. Rearranging the facts doesn't change them. Focusing on one doesn't erase the others. Like the words in a Latin sentence, if you ignore them, you just miss the point.

I believe that each of us has a duty to work to improve those facts. And the core of that is not only an honest, nonlinear understanding of the world, but often a nonlinear approach to the problems. As I have learned through years of playing golf, you can be in the same sand trap on your third stroke, your first stroke, or your tenth stroke. But each time you revisit it, you return with more knowledge.

The problems we have in our world have been revisited countless times. We have found ourselves in the same traps, same woods, and same situations again and again. But I believe that we can improve each time we are there. I hope to use my education to help improve those situations, those facts of the world. I know my path will be as nonlinear and unpredictable as my old note-card stories, but now, as an adult, that path will be guided by an increased awareness of and compassion for the entirety of the human world.

NOTE: The interesting connection is not the primary focus of the essay. It is something added into the essay to make it sound cool. It is also used to create a theme to form the basis of the essay. In this case, the basis is "nonlinearity."

Notice that once I had the idea of nonlinearity, it was just a matter of making up some cool fake story that was about nonlinearity.

Also, in case you're curious, the only part of that essay that is actually true is that my dad is an engineer.

Finding some unusual similarity just gives you an interesting theme to build your essay around. When people write essays, their discussion of reality is usually very superficial. When you find some unusual connection, it allows you to break through the surface of obvious reality. It lets you think about something deeper and more interesting. That deeper, more interesting thing makes the essay worthwhile.

In other words, this isn't a compare and contrast essay. Finding an interesting connection breaks open the obvious surface of reality, and lets you see something worth writing about.

Now let's do another one. This one came from our most recent college strategy seminar:

The attendees picked grass and headphones as two different things.

- The obvious things: both are physical, both are solid.
- Less obvious: both are associated with quietude.

We realized that people often associate being in a field with quietude and tranquility. Many hypnotic inductions begin: "Imagine you are in a field." Headphones are also associated with quietude and tranquility. We also noticed that when listening to a hypnotic, relaxing tape about being in a field, you are often wearing headphones.

We decided to write an essay that turns that on its head. In other words, we decided to begin with making the headphones the thing associated with tranquility, rather than the field. Then, in about 30 minutes, we wrote this quick essay sketch:

"Imagine that you're sitting on a couch, looking at an iPad. You can feel the plastic leather texture of the earcups around your ears, and the near-silent electrical hum that is your definition of silence."

If, in the future, somebody wants to hypnotically bring me to a happy place, that's the induction they'll use. They won't have me imagine being in the middle of a field because I have spent very little time in the middle of fields, and I'm not sure I would find it particularly comforting. My comfort spaces have always been technological: the quietude of headphones, the infinity of Wikipedia, the hallucinatory dreams of YouTube. In a hyper scheduled life of school, soccer, homework, only the monolith of technology seems able to intrude.

In the quietude of this often maligned, technological third space, I have had my own greatest moments of creativity. These third spaces are both uncharted and unchartable. New websites, news articles, and ranking algorithms come and go far too quickly to be properly mapped and known. In that experimental chaos, we are constantly reminded of the unchartable infinity of our own thoughts.

In this dream world, I have created both the successful projects that have withstood the test of time, and those that were as quickly cast away and forgotten as this morning's dream. I was watching Let's Play videos of Call of Duty when I first thought of the idea of Literary Kites, which so massively took off. I was browsing Wikipedia when I thought of the concept of organic scented inks, which, it turns out, are chemically unfeasible.

This technological third space is often seen as antisocial. It is not. It is a place where people share their greatest ideas and most private emotions. It was where I learned that the paralytic social anxiety that I felt was not unusual or shameful. It was also where I learned how to overcome it, both to spread the message of my Literary Kites business to various entrepreneurial competitions, and to learn to speak and share ideas with total strangers, no matter how much it terrified me. And in those conversations, I have learned how to move past the small talk that's so expected in the "offline world", and into the conversations that technology has shown we all crave.

The next journey of my life will be more deeply exploring the uncharted and unchartable territories of human thought. I am drawn to higher education not merely for the academic knowledge, which my third space can provide easily, but for the accidental and unknowable moments of shared intellectual creation that even today are best found face to face.

Note that in a very short time, you can make an effective sketch of a profound sounding essay. The "Literary Kites", by the way, was a sample of an unusual thing we discussed earlier in the seminar. Making Literary Kites would be a thing to help you stand out.

How did we come up with Literary Kites in the first place? We just listed different things, and connected very unrelated things. In this case, it was kites and pencils.

OTHER WAYS TO START THINKING PROFOUNDLY

You can do the opposite of this, by finding similarities between two very closely related things. The non-obvious differences will open an interesting discussion. Similar things could be squids and octopi, iPhones and Androids, SUVs and Pickup Trucks, etc.

You can also Reverse Clichés. That means you take a common saying, and then disagree with it.

For example, if the original saying is "Don't Look a Gift Horse in the Mouth," the reversed saying is "Always Look a Gift Horse in the Mouth." If the original is "Where there is a will, there is a way," it can be reversed to "Where there is a way, there is a will," or "Where there is a will, there is not a way."

You can do this with literally any cliché, proverb, famous quote, etc.

In another college essay seminar, we used spoons and forks as two similar things that we found differences between. Then we added a reversed cliché. Our cliché was, "A watched pot never boils." The reversal of that cliché: An unwatched pot never boils.

The differences between spoons and forks were listed like this:

- Spoons are for kids, forks are for adults.

- Spoons distort reflections.

- Forks are functional and prevent daydreaming.

- Magicians bend spoons, like in the movie *The Matrix*.

Here is the essay:

When I was a little kid, of all my many infuriating habits, the most infuriating was how long it took me to eat. It would take me hours to get through a simple meal. My parents could not understand why my younger sister could finish a bowl of cheerios in less than half the time that I could.

In reality, it wasn't that I was chewing slowly or that I didn't like the food. I was lost in my spoon. Literally. The second my mom turned her back I was gazing at the distorted, magical reflections of my nostril, the inner eye, the underside of my lip.

The worst day of my childhood was when my mom figured out what was going on and made me switch to a fork. My two-sided, reversible, spherical mirror was replaced with the flat, broken planes of a fork. I made a good effort to try to make the fork work. I tried to use the curved portion between the handle and the tines, but it wasn't the same. While the fork was curved, it was only a cylinder, not a sphere.

While the physical spoon left me at age 6, its abstract version remained a part of my life. While my class focused on the main themes in an English story, I would find myself lost in some "minor" detail, some surprising description, some clever analogy. For most of elementary school, although I loved to read and write, my English grades and performance reports were embarrassing. The sports field told a similar story. In soccer, I would be too lost in the angles of attacking and passing, the distance between my foot and the ball, to be much of an athlete.

My mom always told me that a watched pot never

boils. As you might have guessed, I was the kid who would stare at the pot, waiting for the tiny bubbles to become giant balloons. But in my own life I have seen that only a watched pot boils. Like Schrodinger's Cat, the skills and abilities that matter only exist when they are most intensively observed. Soon my habit of watching myself watch the ball, or watching myself get lost in some random part of a book made new abilities come into being. By eighth grade, I had a new spoon: a lacrosse stick. And in school, my new implement was my retractable, purple, sparkly gel ink pen. The hours of fixating on "irrelevant" angles in soccer and on the "trivial" details in books had started to pay off. By eighth grade I was my lacrosse team's lead scorer and I was the president of the Literary Magazine.

This ability to see what other people ignore has paid off the most in community service. At the nursing home that I volunteer at, I noticed that the residents were extremely unhappy with the angle of the television in the common area. Because of that, they would often avoid socializing with other residents, instead turning toward medically dangerous isolation. After we adjusted this, the number of people spending time in the common area dramatically increased and socialization was improved.

I spent my childhood having my face studied and

distorted by spoons. I'd like to return the favor. I want to learn to shape social reality the way that stage magicians bend spoons. I've learned from writing, lacrosse, and service that those who can see the small details can change the entire outcome. I've learned the importance of not just watching the details, but watching myself watch the details. I've learned the importance of listening to others describe the details that they see, that I might miss. I want to study semiotics in a way that allows me to study the historicity of the communities that our current modes of thinking have overlooked. Just as I have lost myself in the details of books and spoons in ways that have shown me what I would never have otherwise seen, I am ready to challenge both external social assumptions and my own deepest preconceptions.

Any intellectual inquiry requires a few important components. You need your analytical knives and the forks of your decision trees. But as every five-year-old knows, no table is complete without a spoon.

Like the previous essay, this essay was sketched out in about 30 minutes. If you are thinking strategically and using these techniques, you can get to a first draft quickly. It might take you longer than it takes me, but it can be done in a few days.

You'll notice that in many essays we make up some childhood story. That's generally used to allow us to create a hero-myth feel to the essay. It's not necessary, but it often works. I have had students who succeeded with a fake childhood story, and students who succeeded without one.

In this essay sketch, I showed the attendees that you can put in some of your achievements and make a good essay. But in general, you don't want to make a laundry list of your achievements. Your essay can highlight your key standout focal point of your application. But it should not just list your resume.

Your parents, by the way, will want you to do that. That approach is wrong. A laundry list of achieve-ments will make you look shallow, uncreative, and weak.

Your parents may suggest creating an essay that is like a laundry list once removed. They might suggest an essay where you describe going through your garage, and how each item there reminds you of some award or achievement you got. That's wrong.

Your personal statement should show who you are. If you are passionate about something specific, that passion is part of who you are. If you are listing 50 awards, then that does not show who you are. That does not show your passion or personality.

Obviously, when I say "show who you are," I mean create a personality portrait of the socialist dimwit that you are pretending to be, because that's what colleges want.

UNIVERSITY ESSAYS

Most elite universities will ask you a question like, "Why do you want to attend college at __________." For most people, this question seems totally insane. What non-obvious reason is there to want to go to an Ivy League college?

But as you've seen throughout this book, colleges are looking for a very specific type of person to fill their dorms and classes. They are trying to determine if you are someone with genuine, hippy-dippy, annoyingly positive, nerdy, academic, socially justified, scientifically curious goals - or just someone with selfish, elitist goals. The way you answer the Why Us? question helps them determine that.

WRONG: Discuss how getting into that college will give you more access to advantage, money, political power, etc.

RIGHT: Answer like someone motivated by stuff other than prestige and advantage.

You should always talk about a specific major you're interested in, one to three specific professors and their research, and at least one specific resource center or program (e.g. an entrepreneurial center or something). It's also good to discuss a particular extracurricular club at that university.

To put the icing on the cake, it's good to quote a particular professor from the department you're interested in. It should probably be the head of the department, or a full tenured professor. Don't quote an assistant or associate professor; that would be like quoting a temporary White House janitor rather than a president.

It doesn't need to be a very specific quote. Instead, find a general quote that can form a good opening or conclusion for the essay. The quote could be something like "We must consider that the previous assumptions were wrong." It should not be, "The CM-7 protein, when activated by the 9-8 modified kinase, appears to have some relevance to Momiroa Syndrome in its earliest phases."

To get the quote, skim through some publications of the professor. Don't quote from the first page of their website, but rather from a book or journal article. You don't have to actually read it. You just need to skim through until you find a usable quote.

Getting specific does two things. First, it shows

that you have researched the details of the college.

(NOTE: you don't need to spend a bunch of time actually doing this. Just do enough to make it seem like you researched the details.)

Second, it shows that you are the type of person who is motivated by the academic, research, and cultural considerations of a college, rather than just by your own personal gain. A purely selfish person only wants to go to Harvard for the name and the quality of the education. The kind of sycophants they're looking for wants to do research, explore social justice nonsense, etc. They are looking for people who will work to help the world, to advance the boundaries of human understanding, etc. (You, like me, are probably more interested in helping yourself, and advancing yourself.)

Consider the "Why do you want to go here" essay to be primarily a personality test. The way you answer tells them if you are the kind of goody-goody approval dog that they want, or the kind of alpha badass that they fear.

One nice thing to add is a childhood story that adds to your motivation. If you, a friend, or a family member had some particular difficulty, for example, then you can open by talking about how that difficulty motivated you to want to study whatever. For example, if you grew up in a place without clean water, you can talk about how that drives your interest in studying chemical engineering under Professor So-And-So, whose research focuses on using polymers to create clean water sources.

Here's a simple example of what an essay can look like:

My parents grew up in Changmoi, a predominantly Chinese and Taiwanese section of Namataba, Uganda. This "Slantytown" was not particularly oppressed in any classical economic way. In fact, the average income in Changmoi is higher than in the rest of Namataba, and also higher than in Kampala, the capital and wealthiest city.

However, my parents considered themselves second class citizens. They've said as much to me, and their stories from back "home" were always colored by a sense of unwantedness and cultural subordination. But despite their best efforts, they couldn't explain to their "artsy" child what the source of that subordination was.

I can't pretend to understand exactly what my parents felt in Namataba. As a second-generation Ugandan-Chinese immigrant, I've felt that sense of cultural subordination, but not in the same way nor to the same degree.

But on my first trip there, at age 14, I started to understand at least one part of it – largely because of my artistic proclivities which my parents have never fully embraced. Namataba is a city of bold, bright colors. This is common in tropical cultures, because "sophisticated" pastels all look white in bright sunlight. All parts of Namataba, including the area where my parents grew up, are decorated in bold colors. The Chinese restaurants and clothing stores have signs just as bright as those anywhere else in the city. That may be the result of economic Darwinism, since restaurants with pastel signs would go unnoticed.

However, at the personal level, things change. Chinese adults and children wear colors far more muted than their native Ugandan counterparts. Pink dresses instead of red, sky blue ties instead of bright blue ones, etc. The colors reflect a culture of polite silence, that may be subordinating itself.

My interest in Yale derives from my interest in how visual and symbolic elements contribute to social power structures, cultural inclusion, and personal identity. I'm most strongly interested in Professor Otang's work on visual hierarchy, which focuses on how very subtle visual cues connote both status and class level. For example, what cues can tell if an empty restaurant would be friendly to people of color?

I also hope to explore these ideas through Yale's Semiotics club. I have had the opportunity to correspond with Jeremy Yepple, the current outreach coordinator of the club, on some of his ideas on how class affects interpretation of visual cues. For example, we discussed how identical visual cues are interpreted differently by people with identical economic statuses but different social classes.

Both the formal research and informal conversations have drawn me to Yale. I currently hope to study semiotics and visual theory, but I want to be in a culture in which people discuss the interplay between such analyses and biology, history, political science, etc. I want to see if and how semiotics applies to biology and ancient philosophy, and how those disciplines affect semiotics. As Professor Otang said in the Journal of Visual Theory, *"Semiotics is the study of signs and how they are psychologically interpreted… but the physical systems are relevant."*

That culture of discussion and interplay across disciplines and not-yet-disciplines draws me to Yale. It is a place where entire methods of understanding the world are born, developed, and debated. I hope to join that process that advances the boundaries of our way of understanding the world.

Okay, here are the important notes on that. First, observe how the essay suggests that the applicant will actually talk to other people. The last thing an Ivy wants is a person who hides in the library and contributes nothing to the discussion. The actual academics at Ivy League colleges are about the same as at community colleges (generally slightly worse). However, the intellectual culture of debate and discussion sets them apart, or so they think. In reality, most of the discussion is about drugs or social justice, so it's not really that valuable either.

Second, observe that the applicant has some clear idea of the desired study. He's not "undecided". Undecided is the most popular major. Given that your goal is to stand out, don't choose undecided. Other popular majors are biology, economics, and political science. These majors are popular because they are used as pre-med, pre-business, and pre-law. I generally recommend avoiding them, unless you've come up with some really compelling story about why you want to study them.

EXAMPLE OF COMPELLING REASON: "My grandparents were political refugees, and I want to study political science to understand and improve the status of political refugees."

EXAMPLE OF NON-COMPELLING REASON: "I want to go to an awesome law school, become a lawyer, and then buy a Ferrari."

Note: obviously becoming a lawyer and buying a Ferrari is actually a good idea. It's just not the idea that the socialist poltroons in the admissions office want to hear.

Dictator Saddam Hussein used to have giant pictures of himself put around Iraq. This is a common practice among dictators. Interestingly, in different parts of the country, the portraits were different, since they were done in the local dress of the region. He realized that by pretending to be one of "the people" in a region, he could manipulate the hapless morons into supporting him. In America, politicians do the same thing. They'll dress and talk differently in rural Texas than in San Francisco, in order to manipulate easy targets into supporting them.

That's what you're doing here. You're manipulating simple-minded people into supporting you by pretending to be one of them. But that doesn't mean it's easy. Political campaigns spend millions of dollars trying to seem like whatever group of uneducated lazies they are targeting at the moment. Take this task of marketing and espionage seriously. Even the tiniest gap in the illusion will bring it crashing down.

For example, let's say a presidential candidate goes to West Virginia and talks about the coal economy, growing research infrastructure, making economic transitions that work, and marrying your cousin. The first three are relevant concerns in West Virginia, while the fourth is a common mocking stereotype about West Virginia. The presence of that last point will totally destroy the illusion that he cares at all about West Virginia.

Espionage takes as much work as preparing for an AP exam. The difference: you can get scores of 5 on 12 AP exams and not get into an Ivy. You can take zero AP exams, use the right espionage, and get in.

INTERVIEWS

When I was applying to colleges, I got into every college where I had a strong interview, and not into the colleges where I had weak interviews. Unfortunately for me, I had more weak interviews than strong ones.

Since then, I've learned a ton about interviews. Some of that comes from my work in education; other parts come from my work in politics. I've trained both students and candidates on how to do interviews, and seen many of the mistakes that you should avoid. I've also made many of the mistakes you should avoid!

Interviews are the hardest parts of espionage. You can't spend six weeks thinking about each sentence. No matter how hard you prepare, there will be questions you just haven't considered before.

In an interview, the non-verbal communication will also matter a lot. The sense a person gets from your nonverbal behaviors – posture, expression, quality of voice, dress, etc. – matters as much as what you actually say.

In an interview, you want to seem confident, intelligent, deep thinking, witty, and relaxed. This isn't easy since you probably feel nervous and terrified! Don't worry, everyone does. You just learn to hide it.

You want to come across as an alpha male or female, an intellectual force of nature, charming because of your ability and confidence. So, let's talk about how to make that illusion happen.

FIRST: DRESS

Your interviewer will probably tell you to dress casually. To you, that may mean shorts and a t-shirt. That is not what it means. "Casual" means business casual. For men, that means dress pants and a button-down shirt. "Formal" means a suit. If someone wants you to wear shorts and a t-shirt, they will say, "Dress like a child."

But remember, your goal is not just to pass the minimum threshold. It's to come across as alpha and dominant. So, go a little farther.

For women: wear a skirt suit or pant suit. You can either wear the jacket or not, up to you. Dress like you take yourself seriously, and your interviewer will take you seriously.

For men: wear a suit jacket or sport coat with a pocket square and a tie if you like. I recommend a full suit, but many men come across well with jeans, a sport jacket, and a pocket square. Since most men avoid any kind of interesting attire, little details will help. For example, look up how to tie a somewhat interesting tie knot or how to fold a pocket square on YouTube. Those details make you come across as a dominant alpha male, rather than a drudge conforming to a dress code. I also recommend a well fitted French cuff shirt and cufflinks.

Among men, some are really into things like cufflinks and pocket squares. If you're wearing them, and your interviewer is of that ilk, you'll have an immediate ally. Other men just don't care. You won't lose anything either way.

As a general rule, it's a good idea to learn to dress well (for both men and women). It's the first thing a person notices about you, and immediately conveys social status. In my own life, when I go to an event wearing a t-shirt (which I often do), people usually assume I'm some random degenerate. If I wear a button-down shirt to a similar event, they assume I'm at least some kind of adult. When I wear a suit, cufflinks, and a pocket square, they often assume

I'm famous. Given that the job of the interviewer is to figure out which people will become famous and let those people in, you can figure out which is the best option.

One PR expert put it very simply: it is impossible to be overdressed. If you want to stand out as someone exceptional, dress exceptionally.

Note: that doesn't necessarily mean you have to dress traditionally though! If you look like a counter-cultural icon, with some crazy hair and all kinds of tattoos and piercings, cool. Go with that. You need to come across as an intense, iconic alpha. It's not necessary to come across as a traditionalist. A blue mohawk can be just as iconic as a suit (although a blue mohawk with a suit is even better).

Final note: make sure your clothes are as form fitting as your body type allows. Any tailor can handle this. If you are muscular or skinny, go on the tight side. If you're super fat, don't worry, a good tailor can turn that to your advantage as well.

I would recommend staying away from loose and flowy clothing. Through all of Western history, upper class men wore tighter, more form fitting clothing. For most of recent Western history, the same has applied to women. Executives don't show up in flowy, hippy, gypsy skirts. They just don't look intense and dominant.

Are there exceptions to these guidelines? Sure. If you're going with the narrative that you are from a struggling, poor family, it would be inexplicable to show up to your interview with cufflinks and a well fitted suit. Dress for whatever part you're playing, obviously. Don't make it weird by dressing up like an 18th century chimney sweep, though.

ARRIVAL AND PREPARATION

Most of the time, you'll meet your interviewer at a coffee shop, their office, or their house. Here's what to do in each circumstance.

If you're meeting at a coffee shop, get there about 45 minutes early and get a seat. About 30 minutes before the interviewer arrives, get a drink of some kind. It can be lemonade, espresso, sparkling water, whatever you like.

Here's why that's important. Most people are too nervous to eat or drink anything. By having a drink, you show that you are calm and confident.

Also, it will help you stand out. Since 99% of people will not have a drink, you'll be a little more memorable just because of that.

Note: it should be some kind of paid drink, not just tap water. If the only thing you like is water, get bottled water. This subtle cue shows social dominance.

However, if you are playing the "struggling family" card, then obviously do not get a paid drink!

Note: many interviewers do several interviews back to back in the same place. When you arrive early, don't call up a friend and say something stupid, or pick a fight with the staff, or something insane. The performance starts as soon as you are within 3 miles of the coffee shop.

You can call a friend and have a non-disgusting conversation, or read a physical book, or a book on your phone. Don't play video games or do anything else equally juvenile.

If you are having a phone conversation, it should not be about the interview! First, you'll almost certainly say something self-incriminating or silly. Second, if you talk about something else, and are overheard, it makes you look unbelievably confident! What type of person would be chatting about a guitar piece or a funny movie right before an Ivy League interview?

I don't recommend getting food, since it's really hard to eat gracefully while doing an interview. Food can get stuck in your teeth, you might accidentally talk with your mouth full, might swallow something weirdly, etc. Also, getting food may be pushing the confidence to a somewhat weird level. Having a drink makes you look relaxed. Ordering a lobster dinner makes you look insane.

Obvious note: no matter how old you are, the drink should not contain alcohol.

THE SMILE

Smiling is a major sign of confidence and social dominance. It also encourages the other person to smile.

Here's the good thing about smiles. You already know that when you feel happy, you smile. But did you know it also works in reverse? When you smile, it makes you feel happy! Also, when you make the other person smile, he feels happy, and has a better "overall impression" of you.

You must learn how to do two types smiles, and be able to use them reliably. For this, it can be useful to work with an acting coach. I have personally worked with April Sigman, who is awesome, and there are many other acting coaches. Beauty pageant coaches, as well as former contestants, can also help with that (they can help both men and women).

The first type of smile is the big, giant, toothy smile. When you first shake hands with someone, or first see someone, that's the smile to use. Practice in front of a mirror or with an acting coach.

The second type of smile is trickier. It's called "smiling with your eyes." In this time of smile, your mouth does very little – maybe a slight upturn. But your eyes do a lot.

It can take some practice to learn how to do it. One method is called "anchoring", in which you remember a happy memory, associate it with a word, and then use that word to recall the happy memory. This makes your eyes "light up", and generally makes the other person also start to feel positive.

You should smile with your eyes pretty much the entire interview, unless you are telling a sad story or something. Even if you are playing the "struggling family" card, still do it. It makes you seem like a rare and magical diamond if you do it. It's like having a halo. It's extremely useful. People don't interpret smiling with your eyes as "being happy", but rather as "having positive energy." Realistically, once you get the hang of it, you should smile with your eyes pretty much all the time. That skill by itself will help you much more in life than any Ivy League degree.

SHAKING HANDS

When you first meet the interviewer, you should make eye contact, smile, and shake hands as follows:

- Hold the other person's hand firmly.

- Move down, then up, then break. Don't shake 20 times. Just down, back up, end.

- Don't grip like you're trying to break the other person's hand, and don't give a dead fish handshake either. If you are a man shaking hands with a woman, your grip should still be firm, but less forceful.

I recommend using a hand strengthener to build up grip strength. This doesn't mean using needless force; if your grip is stronger, then you are in a position to increase force to whatever level is needed. This lets you adjust strength without having to worry about being caught in some weirdly awkward handshake. Some people, instead of starting with their hands flat, start with their hands cupped. This inexplicable habit means that they will be farther ahead in the handshake, often trapping your hands or fingers in an awkward way. If your hands are just much stronger than theirs, it won't be much of an issue.

EYE CONTACT

Make eye contact always. Imagine a triangle created by the eyes and nose of the person. Keep your gaze always within that triangle.

This is, by the way, really hard. When you think, you're going to want to look away for a second to collect your thoughts. That's okay, but not ideal. Even worse is when you look away for too long, and then start to answer while still looking away!

Practice answering questions while making eye contact. It is useful for college interviews, media interviews, Skype interviews, and public speaking.

POSTURE

You know what "good posture" is: chin up, shoulder's back and down, chest out, standing straight.

Interestingly, in many martial arts, the ideal posture is the exact opposite! You keep your chin down so you can't be punched in the chin. You keep your chest caved in, to protect your solar plexus. Your shoulders are up to protect the side of your head.

So, which is the good posture, evolutionarily speaking? How can two opposite postures both be "good"?

As it turns out, what we call "good" posture is good precisely because it is so bad for an actual fight. "Good" posture (chest out, chin up) is a highly vulnerable and unsafe posture. Counterintuitively, vulnerability shows strength.

By not bothering to defend yourself, or even adopt a fighting posture, you are indicating a total lack of fear. This shows extreme confidence. You're saying, "I'm so powerful that I am not afraid of a single thing in the world ever. Nothing is a threat to me."

Because it has so much vulnerability, good posture shows fearlessness.

You should practice both standing and seated posture. Practice sitting up straight, standing up straight, etc. One common practice is to stand against a wall, flatten out your shoulder blades, have your head up and leaning against the wall. Ballet and modern dancers also have other techniques to improve posture. As does the military.

Don't underestimate the power of good posture. It makes you look much more powerful and dominant.

A female friend of mine who had a mom that was very strict about posture often travelled on the Metro in DC. Even though she wore normal civilian clothing, she would at times get saluted by Pentagon employees near that metro stop.

My own posture is nothing extraordinary, but even I've seen the benefits. At one point, I got injured and could not do any upper body workouts for a couple months. During that time, I instead practiced posture relentlessly. Although I had stopped all upper body workouts, everyone asked me if I was working out harder! While my muscle mass was significantly less, my presence was significantly more intense.

For seated posture, there are two schools of thought. Some people say that the small of your back should touch the back of the chair. This prevents slouching.

A more classical school of thought says that no part of your back should touch the back of the chair at all. In the 19th century, governesses would put knives on the backs of the chairs of aristocratic children to help enforce this skill. Leaning against the chair back was seen as a sign of low class weakness. If you've ever sat in an old-time chair, you've noticed how uncomfortable it is to lean against the back. The backs were not for leaning.

There is no school of thought that encourages slouching, however. Slouching just looks weak.

VOCAL CONTROL, VOCAL VARIETY

Remember how a vulnerable posture conveys fearlessness, and therefore strength? The same is true of voice! Just as an "open" posture conveys fearlessness, an "open" voice also conveys fearlessness.

Most teenagers speak in monotones. This shows nothing but fear. Speaking in a monotone prevents you from revealing any emotions. That means that you are afraid that the other person will know your emotions.

When adults are being interrogated by the police, they often speak in monotones. They don't want to reveal anything, so they hide everything in their voice. If you've seen any prison shows, you've seen that most prisoners speak in monotones when talking to guards.

In your own life, you've been mostly in a position of powerlessness. You've been seeking approval from teachers, so they'll write you good recommendations. You've been pretending to think community service projects are not super boring and pointless, so you can get approval from those running them, or get some award, or whatever. You've learned to hide your true emotions, and there is a roughly 100% chance you currently speak in a monotone. (If you've done a lot of vocal training for acting or singing, then you might not.)

So now it's time to learn to show your true emotions.

Just kidding. That idea would be completely insane. Showing your true emotions is never a part of college strategy, or any other strategy. Instead, we are going to create the illusion of vocal openness!

To achieve this, you must learn vocal variety. That means you will have your voice vary a lot. Sometimes you'll talk fast, sometimes, slow, sometimes with a high pitch, sometimes with a low pitch, sometimes soft, sometimes loud.

You'll learn to do it deliberately, and be in control of it.

When you speak in a monotone, it shows fear. But when you have a lot of vocal variety it shows power. Now you need to learn to manufacture vocal variety, to create this illusion.

If you have access to a voice or acting coach, ask for help with these exercises. If not, you can do them with a friend, a parent, or voice recorder on your phone or computer.

Exercise 1: Speed

In the first exercise, you will learn how to vary the speed of your speech. Pick up any book. Then read it with huge variations in speed.

The variations should be really, ridiculously exaggerated. The goal is to stretch the range of your ability. If the sentence is:

"The fat dog ran."

You might read it like

"Theeeeeeeeeeeeeeeeeeeeeeeeee fat dooog raaa aaaaaaaaaaaaaaaaaaaaaaaaaaaaaaaaaaaaaaa aaaaaaaaaaaaaaaaaaaaaaaaaaaaaaaan."

Make the fast parts ridiculously fast. Make the slow parts ridiculously slow.
Practice this a lot.

Exercise 2: Basic Pitch

Now we'll do the same with pitches. Read a book out loud. Vary your pitch from as high as you can possibly go to as low as you can possibly go. Go from a mouse squeak to Darth Vader, and everything in between.
Practice that a lot, with a coach, friend, family member, or computer.

Exercise 3: Combining Speed and Pitch

For the next exercise, practice varying both speed and pitch!

Exercise 4: Rising, Falling, and Level Pitches

Some people speak in a constant rising pitch. It makes everything sound like a question. It sounds weak and uncertain. It's like this:

My friend and I? Like went to the mall? And we purchased a shirt?

The opposite is a falling pitch. It makes everything sound like a command. It shows power:

My friend. And I. Went to the store.

In fact, asking a question with a falling pitch shows even more power.

Instead of: "Do you want to study art?"

You can use: "Do you want to study art."

This subtle change will make you sound more authoritative and in control.

In this exercise, you will practice using falling tones and rising tones. Say some words with rising tones, and others with a falling tone. You can make them very exaggerated. Make the falling tones like:

YESTERday I DEVoured a HIPpo.

Do the reverse for rising tones.

Note that there is not one "right pitch". The goal is to have variety. Mix things up. The more variation you show, the more power you convey. Your default, though, should probably be a falling pitch. This sounds commanding and powerful. It's the opposite of the common and weak rising pitch.

Exercise 5: Volume

In addition to varying speed and pitch, you should be able to vary volume. Practice varying from a whisper to a booming voice.

Exercise 6: Mixed Exercise

Practice varying speed, pitch, and volume a lot while you read a passage.

NOW SEE AN EXAMPLE

On YouTube, look up "Star Trek, First Duty." You should see some a 3-4 minute video from *Star Trek: The Next Generation*.

In this scene, you see two professional actors who have studied voice extensively. One actor speaks in a monotone on purpose to show fear. The other uses a huge amount of vocal variety to show dominance. Listen to the huge changes in speed, pitch, and volume.

If you listen carefully, you'll hear falling, rising – and even falling-rising and rising-falling tones!

Optional Advanced Exercise

Timbre means the quality of your voice. Anger, happiness, and sadness all produce different timbres.

Try practicing different timbres. Anger is the easiest emotion to fake, followed by happiness. Sadness is harder.

More advanced emotions are also good to practice with a partner. You might try "holding back panic", "slightly confused", "relieved", etc.

It takes much longer to learn that, but it's worth it. However, just by mastering speed, pitch, and volume, you can massively improve your vocal presence.

The most important tool of all of them is speed. Varying your speed is the simplest way to introduce vocal variety. At the very least, you can use it to prevent yourself from talking too fast, which shows nervousness.

GESTURES

Go ahead and rewatch the First Duty video. You see that the monotone boy remains still, while the vocally powerful captain moves all over the whole room! Just as monotone shows weakness, fear of motion also shows weakness.

People ask what the "right" type of gesture is. The answer: it doesn't really matter. You can use pretty much any kind of gesture at all. If you do it with control and confidence, it works.

To use gestures effectively, you need to understand some regions of personal space.

Suppose you are sitting across a small table from another person. Your immediate personal space is about a foot around you. The half of the table closer to you is your assigned space. The other half of the table is the other person's assigned space. Within a foot of the other person is that person's personal space.

A gesture within your personal space is polite.

Breaking out of your personal space and into your assigned space is dramatic.

Breaking into the other person's personal space is invasive.

Most people don't move at all during an interview. This shows fear. You should freely move within your personal and assigned space. You can move your hands freely in those regions.

Only if you want to make a major point should you break into the other person's assigned space.

In a college interview, never break into the other person's personal space! Save that either for flirting with or threatening someone, neither of which applies to the college interview.

But don't hide inside your assigned personal space like a turtle. Show confidence and charisma by breaking boundaries.

One nice technique is to use a gesture that brings an arm sideways out of your personal space. You can reach as far to the right or left as you like. That allows you to break out of your personal space safely, without moving toward the interviewer at all.

WHAT TO TALK ABOUT

An interview is not a pop quiz. It's a conversation that you can control. You must learn to direct the conversation to your strengths and highlights.

What should you talk about? The things that make you stand out. You probably have them in your application.

For example, I don't know much about professional sports, since I find them excruciatingly boring. But I do know about books, because I am a huge nerd. In a social conversation or interview, if sports come up, I use a transition like this: "Speaking of <insert name of sports thing here>, did you guys ever hear of the book Moneyball?"

If they say yes, I'll then direct the conversation to being about books, perhaps by asking, "Do you like to read nonfiction books like that?" If they say no, I'll just ask what kind of books they like to read.

CONTROLLING THE CONVERSATION: NON-SEQUITURS

Take a look at this conversation:

You: I'm Hungry

Your Friend: I know a Chinese restaurant that's open until 10.

If a robot analyzed this, the robot would determine that your friend is a horrible person! You told your friend that you were hungry. Your friend ignored you, and decided to instead brag about his knowledge of local businesses.

Of course, as humans we understand that the apparent non-sequitur was actually intended as a solution to the problem.

In fact, it would have been super weird and awkward if your friend had said this:

"I understand and acknowledge that you are hungry. Might I suggest as a solution to your hunger, we go to a location that can provide food, which will cure your hunger. One place we can go is a particular Chinese restaurant. It is open late enough for us to get there before it closes."

The same is true of college interviews, and even of college counselor questionnaires! You can easily work any conversation or question to your strong suit, and the counsellor or interviewer won't even think it's weird.

Suppose the interviewer asks, "Do you have any siblings?"

You can say, "Yes, I have a younger sister who works with me on my poetry kite business."

No one asked about the kite business. The only logical answers to "Do you have any siblings" are "Yes" or "No". But bringing in the extra information doesn't come across as weird at all.

Don't treat your interview or questionnaire as a pop quiz where you just wait to be asked questions. Think of it instead as a conversation that you will lead to your strengths.

INTERESTING ANSWERS

Some interviewers will ask general questions to get to know you. These will be questions like, "What historical figure do you identify with," or "What's your favorite movie."

Your answer doesn't have to be true. It has to be interesting.

Suppose the interviewer asks what your favorite historical figure is. Let's also assume that George Washington happens to be your favorite historical figure. Too bad. You can't say that. It makes you look like a simpleton.

Instead, just pick any historical figure you know about, who is not some obvious cliché. Don't pick someone known to be negative, like Hitler or Stalin. People like Voltaire, Euclid, and Martha Graham are all in the right range. Just whoever you did your last report on, even if that was in 5th grade, is a perfectly fine choice (as long as the report wasn't on Abraham Lincoln).

If they ask you your favorite book, don't say Harry Potter, even if that is your favorite book. Don't say the most popular book in your school. Pick something interesting (that you've actually read and can discuss, obviously).

If they ask your favorite movie, don't pick something that makes you look like a moron, like

Transformers 4. Find a classic or independent movie. If you've never seen a movie with any brains, look at lists of top independent or classical movies, and watch 2-5 of them.

If you can't think of something interesting, just say something, and get excited about it. If the only historical figure you can think of is George Washington, then talk passionately about how reading about George Washington inspired you to <do whatever unique activity is the showpiece of your application>.

WRONG: Ummm...I guess George Washington.

RIGHT: George Washington really inspired me to start making Jack O Lanterns out of mangoes to support refugees.

Suppose you can't think of a book.

WRONG: Maybe...The Cat in the Hat?

RIGHT: The Cat in the Hat is one of my favorites, it's a major part of why I want to work to end censorship in China.

Realistically, before the interview, it's probably wise to decide what some of your favorites are going to be, and think through them a bit. Then you can pretend to think about it for a second during the interview, but you won't feel panicked.

HOSTILE INTERVIEWS

Sometimes you'll get a really hostile interviewer who challenges everything you say. Good news: that usually means you're going to get in to that college, as long as you withstand the interview!

Think of it like this: would you aggressively debate with a person with a developmental disability like Downs Syndrome? Probably not, since that would be messed up even by my standards. Similarly, interviewers won't aggressively attack applicants they see as weak. They'll just be polite to them.

If you get a really hostile interviewer, that means that he thinks you're at a high level. He thinks it's totally okay to attack you, which means he respects you.

Here's what you need to do:

1. Keep your cool no matter what. Talk slowly, calmly. Consider your answers.

2. Don't back down. The interviewer is testing your bravery and perseverance. Don't back down no matter how hard he attacks. Just politely debate back.

Unless you're the smartest and most alpha person in the world ever, you probably won't get more than one or two hostile interviews. If you get more, congratulations.

At Vohra, we specifically practice hostile interviews. You can do that with a friend or family member. Have them attack you mercilessly, and just hold your ground and fight back. Don't yell or swear. The interviewer is testing your resolve, calm, and perseverance.

It's perfectly fine to gently provoke a hostile interview. To do that, just bring forth a somewhat controversial activity. For example, if I want to provoke a hostile political interview, I might say something like, "The Libertarian Party's major goal is to eliminate all public schools." (I am currently the Vice Chair of the Libertarian party.) If I want to provoke a friendly interview, I might say, "The Libertarian Party wants to promote freedom for all people, all of the time."

You can do something similar with anything.

Friendly Provocation: "I love playing the violin."

Hostile Provocation: "Violin has been more important to me than any school class. I've started an organization to replace math education with music education."

The interviewer will almost certainly take the bait, unless he's actively avoiding taking the bait.

Friendly Provocation: I loved playing soccer as a kid.

Hostile Provocation: I love soccer, but I believe that all scoring should be removed from all sports.

Get the idea? Interviewers usually do several interviews, and generally forget all of them. But they won't forget the provocative ones. It's much better to be opposed and hated than forgotten. Pretty much everyone who attends an Ivy League college believes that welcoming opposing views is necessary. They won't oppose you just because they disagree with you...unless you come off as racist, sexist, homophobic, etc.

Obviously, your controversial views cannot target any group in a negative light. Find something that's politically correct, but will invite opposition.

One student recently had an exceptionally hostile interview. At the end of the interview, the interviewer told the student that no other student had actually managed to withstand his interviewing style! The student obviously got in.

MEMORABLE QUESTIONS

What's better than giving a memorable answer? Asking a memorable question! Most interviewers will give you an opportunity to ask questions at the end of the interview. That's a time to shine.

Finding the right question can be tough. It shouldn't be so obvious that you can get the answer from the website. It shouldn't be a hyper specific question more appropriate for a google search than an interview.

Good questions to ask the interviewer at that point are:

- What surprised you about your experience?
- What course inspired you the most? What was it like?
- What was your most inspiring professor like?

Here are some from PrepScholar.com:

- What advice would you have for an incoming freshman?
- What do you wish you knew while you were a freshman?
- What do you wish you knew while you were in college?
- I read about (some tradition). Have you participated? What's it like?

Those will work fine for a generic approach. Now here's some that combine the strategy of standing out with something unusual.

Suppose you are claiming to be an entrepreneur, making philosophy t-shirts (or actually are doing it. After all, being an entrepreneur is actually a good idea.) You can ask:

- "Did you know any entrepreneurs who were able to play club or varsity sports? Do you think it would be realistic with the course load?"

- "Did you know any entrepreneurs who were able to double major?"

If you are claiming to be a person really passionate about some bit of history, philosophy, or whatever:

- "Did you know anyone who wrote a book while in school? Do you think there would be people who could provide some guidance?"
- "Did the TV/Radio station ever do short documentaries?"

If you are about being an avante-garde artist:

- "Does the university do student art exhibits? Did you know anyone who did gallery exhibits while at school?"

Things to avoid asking:

- "Are the people attractive?"
- "Are the parties fun?"
- "What are my odds of getting in?"
- "Can you put in a good word for me?"
- "Which is the best program at the school?"

In other words: you don't want to seem like a hedonist or like someone in a simpleminded rat race. You should come across as someone passionate and excited, not someone trying to simplistically get ahead. Obviously, getting ahead is perfectly fine, it just doesn't come across well in an interview.

Everyone on earth wants to get ahead. Not everyone is passionate about something unusual. Creating the illusion (or reality) of that passion helps you stand out.

Do not ask about rankings of any kind. Do not ask about your chances of getting in at all.

ADVANCED TECHNIQUES

Some of you reading this are highly gregarious, confident people. If that's you, here are a couple advanced methods to consider. The goal of these methods is to turn the interview into a close conversation, to make the interviewer feel a deep sense of connection with you, to feel like he's talking to a close friend. If you're unsure or hesitant, you can skip these. These are advanced techniques.

We speak to our close friends very differently than we speak to strangers. With strangers, we talk about one thing at a time. With friends, we talk about multiple things at the same time. Friends often have about 3 conversations happening at the same time.

Conversations are also two-way, whereas interviews are generally mostly one way. In a traditional interview, the interviewer asks questions, and you answer. In a conversation, the questions go both ways.

Establishing the Two-way Conversation

First, as soon as realistically possible, ask the interviewer some question about himself. For example, if you meet in a law office, you can ask what kind of law he does, how long he's been at that office, etc. The question should come across as innocuous, like harmless small talk. If you meet at a coffee shop, you can ask the interviewer if he is more of a coffee person or a tea person. Just ask it casually, while you're shaking hands, or sitting down, or something.

The goal is to establish a precedent in which you are allowed to ask questions. All conversations have unspoken rules, usually established right at the beginning of the interaction between two people. If you can make it okay for you to ask questions, you can turn the interview into a two-way conversation.

The next phase is to open multiple conversation threads. When you are talking with a friend, you might be simultaneously discussing where to eat, someone you're attracted to, a TV show, and a car. The conversation threads are all open at the same time. But with a stranger, you end one conversation topic before starting the next.

To force an interview into that mode, you basically need to just interrupt yourself and create a new topic mid answer. It's like this:

"I learned the most from my chemistry teacher, because we did these projects-- Have you seen the documentary about the discovery of gunpowder?"

By interrupting yourself, now you have created two open conversations. You're now talking about some yet undescribed projects, and also a documentary. It's gone from a sequential conversation, the type you use with strangers, to a parallel conversation, the kind you use with friends. Obviously, the documentary should connect back and help you close both conversations at some point, otherwise you'll look scattered. As long as they connect, you can self-interrupt all day long, creating more and more open threads.

"I really like my soccer team because we use the Sierra Nevada system, and – have you heard about that system?"

Don't interrupt the interviewer though. That's generally considered rude.

Creating Psychological Investment

The next phase of this is to get him to psychologically invest in you. This requires getting him to share something personal. It's easier in a purely social setting, but you can do it in an interview if you're up to it. Here's how it works. You need to get the interviewer to talk about his childhood. You can't just go right for it, like "TELL ME ABOUT YOUR CHILDHOOD." That will seem insane and serial-killery. Instead, it's like this:

"A lot of my interest in art comes from being a middle child – do you have any siblings?" At that point, you've shown trust by telling the interviewer about your childhood. At this point, if he refuses to answer, he'll come across as the serial killer, so he'll usually answer.

Why does this matter? Psychologically, if you've invested in something, you're more likely to commit to it. If you've invested $5000 in one project, and $2 in another, and one has to go, it's the $2 one. You'll keep the one you invested in.

By the way, this is bad economics. You should only consider which will bring more future profit. However, human nature is powerful, and people stick to what they've invested in. You can use this to your advantage. If the interviewer has invested in you by sharing personal details, and not similarly invested in someone else, that other person is going to be swept into the dustbin of history.

You know that when you feel happy, you smile. But it also works in reverse. When you smile, your brain thinks you are happy.

Similarly, you share more about yourself with

people you like. And in the reverse, if you share more about yourself with a person, your brain assumes you must like them.

You can gradually increase the personal nature of the questions to build rapport. For example, you can say, "My first art piece was about this totally ragged stuffed bunny I had. I called him Mr. Bunny- Did you ever have one of those sentimental but ugly childhood toys?"

Great stage magicians know not to use a trick in public until its ready. Before you use it in an interview, use it in social settings – with friends of the family, with strangers, at social gatherings, just wherever. These techniques are awesome when done smoothly, but jarringly weird if you've never practiced them.

FIRST GENERATION

Colleges are in love with people who are the first people in their families to go to college. If neither of your parents went to college, you're in luck.

If your parents went to college in a different country, and are entrepreneurs not professionals, then you're also in luck. For example, if your dad went to the most famous college in all of China, and he now runs a small business, just have him strip that part out of his biography. However, if is a lawyer, doctor, or something else that legally requires a college degree, that won't work.

Parents: if you are considering having kids, and one of you never went to college, here's what to do. First, get legally divorced. Then have kids, and make the non-college person the legal full parent. You don't actually change anything about your life, just the paperwork.

If both your parents went to U.S. colleges, then there's not much you can do.

ALTERNATIVES TO AMERICAN SCHOOLS

BRITISH COLLEGES

Oxford and Cambridge are easily as prestigious as Harvard and Yale. The difference: getting in simply requires high academic skill, not a willingness to kowtow to social justice idiocy.

Applying to a British college is very different from applying to an American one. First, you aren't applying for a generalist program. You are applying to a specific field of study (as you would in an American graduate school). If you apply to study chemistry, then you're going to study chemistry, be interviewed about chemistry, etc.

British colleges are much cheaper than American ones. On the other hand, if you are an American, you won't get much or any financial aid. If you're rich enough that you'll have to pay full price in

America, you'll save by going to Britain. If you'll be getting a bunch of financial aid in the U.S., it may make the U.S. college cheaper.

When you apply to Oxford and Cambridge, here's what to expect.

First, you need to have a 1500+ SAT score, 5s on the relevant AP exams, and 750+ on the relevant SAT subject tests. British citizens take exams called the A levels, which stands for Advanced Levels. They are like AP exams (although, in my view, much easier). Americans can substitute AP exams.

You will also have a very intimidating interview. Your job: don't get intimidated. Stay calm.

The interview will not be a U.S. style, "what's your favorite type of dog" interview. Instead, it will be questions and problems about the subject you intend to study. If you plan to study math, expect some hard math problems that you will have to do live.

The interviewers will intentionally mess with you, by checking their watches, acting like they think you are mildly retarded, etc. That's part of the test. Just keep your cool. Feel free to ask the interviewers questions about the problem, or about the question they are asking.

You will have to prepare seriously for the interview. But you won't have to waste time doing community service at nursing homes to fill your resume.

Your essays will be a bit more straightforward than the ones you would use for American colleges. You'll talk clearly about your early inspirations, recent achievements, and eventual goals in that specific subject. You'll explain why that subject moves you. Feel free to make a few interesting analogies, or even bring in an interesting quote. Focus also on the specific programs at the school to which you are applying.

The interview and your standardized test scores will matter more than the essay.

SUPERIOR ALTERNATIVES TO ANY COLLEGE

Commercials for pretty much any consumer good will try to convince you that the product is either necessary or extremely beneficial. That doesn't make it true.

The product could be needless, or there might be some better option.

If you're seriously considering an Ivy League college, it means you are already independently academically motivated. That means, you already have the ability to learn material on your own.

If you can't, I have bad news for you: you'll have to. Much of the teaching at Ivy League colleges is so terrible that you have no choice but to learn it on your own.

When considering alternatives to college, you need to carefully consider what you're trying to get from college. You're probably looking for personal advantage. Maybe you want to improve your critical thinking abilities and creative abilities, or increase your likelihood of financial success. You probably want social prestige, as well as a way to prove your ability to employers.

Are there better ways to do that without college?

Let's start with the simplest question: how can you prove to employers that you have the academic ability they want? In many areas, you can prove those abilities with very difficult standardized tests. In math, you can take the first Actuarial Exam, which is a test of calculus and statistics. If you pass it, it can greatly increase your odds of getting a financial sector job. To prove ability in the humanities and general knowledge, consider the Foreign Service Officer's Test. This test is used by the State Department for those who want to become diplomats. It is also widely recognized as a test of impressive skill, and can open doors that even an Ivy League degree cannot.

In medicine, while most MD schools require that you first squander 4 years and $200k on an undergraduate program, many DO schools do not. They just want to make sure your MCAT score is high enough. Independent study can get you there. Then, the type of doctor you become is based pretty much entirely on your Step 1 board score. This is an extremely difficult standardized test. If your score is high enough, you can get into a highly paid medical field and do a residency at a prestigious university. In medicine, you learn almost all of the important stuff during your residency, not in MD or DO school.

Law is trickier. Virginia allows you to "read for the law", as Abraham Lincoln did. About 30 or so people a year pass the Bar exam in Virginia without wasting money on law school, but you still have to squander time and money on an undergraduate degree.

But let's have the real discussion now. You're probably telling people you want to go to college to become a lawyer, doctor, or some other such professional. Is that what you really want?

Many who claim they want to be a lawyer actually want to be a congressman or president. They noticed that many politicians are lawyers, so they think they need to be one too. But the only reason that so many are lawyers is that so many who want to be politicians thought they had to be lawyers first! Many politicians have skipped that step. Plenty of legislators and congressman never graduated from college at all.

You can get involved in politics without taking such an insanely circuitous route. You need to work on public speaking, learn the inner workings of the party of your choice, and get involved directly in that party. Be bold, outspoken, and noticeable, but study the culture carefully first. See what type of messaging works in that culture.

If you're claiming to want to be a doctor, my guess is you probably like science and money. Consider launching product ideas on Kickstarter or interning at innovative companies. Interning tip: if you want to rise in the ranks of a small, innovative company, show up early every day. Companies think that young people are lazy, unreliable, entitled, drunken, deadbeats. They usually are, thanks to the toxic cultures of college and public school. But if you are sober, timely, and hard-working, you'll stand out immediately.

If you're undecided, chances are you probably don't want to be limited by one thing, and want an exciting life of new possibilities and successes. Consider starting a small business. Realistically, consider starting several businesses, since most new businesses fail (even when the founder has a college degree). The world of entrepreneurship is far more exciting, changing, lucrative, and fun than the corporate rat race.

Don't believe me? I recommend reading the Communist Manifesto, in which Karl Marx explains that in capitalism, capitalists (business owners) benefit and laborers get shafted. You can also read the many articles on "white collar slavery", in which people with high education levels are stuck doing tedious, uncreative labor for bare survival wages. Watch the movie *Office Space*, if you haven't already, for a more humorous analysis of corporate life. You'll soon realize that running a small business has many advantages over being a low level nothing in a big one.

Then, I recommend looking at the positives of what real, self-driven entrepreneurship can look like. I found the fictional account in *The Fountainhead* very inspiring. Others have found that biographies of famous entrepreneurs and CEOS give them good direction. Consider the biographies or autobiographies of people whose products you like - Nike, Apple, Chanel, etc. You'll see that trailblazers and innovators think differently, unapologetically, and without need for approval from authority. You'll see how they overcame obstacles, and especially how they overcame fear.

If you want to be a writer, awesome. I recommend learning about Ray Bradbury, who specifically avoided college and chose to use the library instead.

Writing professionally requires the ability to self-motivate. You won't learn that in college.

Richard Branson, Ralph Lauren, Steve Jobs, Mark Zuckerberg, and Bill Gates show that you can be a billionaire without college. But there are many more people who had more modest success without college. I just learned that a friend's younger brother bought a house at 19. He didn't start Facebook or anything. He just manages a carwash and saves money. While many college graduates are paying off college debt into their 50s and 60s, he just decided not to get duped. He didn't need to be a tech genius. He just needed to not be a totally gullible buffoon who thinks that a degree in Social Justice is worth $200K. Given a chance between being psychologically manipulated or not, he chose not.

Maybe you're interested in graphic design. Practice, read, learn, and compete. Go on 99designs.com, and try to win some design contests. Even if you never win, you'll be getting a real education in design and business, and you won't have to spend $200K. Keep reading, studying, and learning. You don't need anyone's approval.

Want to learn by competing elsewhere? Consider elance.com or fiverr.com. You'll see what a hyper competitive market looks like, and learn that you can earn money without being someone else's approval dog. You probably won't make much money on Fiverr, but it's a low-cost way to get an introduction into the awesome jungle that is the free market.

As you keep trying new things, you'll come to understand what education really looks like. You'll read books to get knowledge to help you with what you are doing, not just to write what a teacher wants to see on a silly English paper. You've always heard that knowledge is power. In the free market, you'll learn how true that is. You'll see how valuable what you learn from books actually is. You'll want every advantage over your competitors. The knowledge in nonfiction books, and the perspective in fiction and literature will take on heightened importance.

It's often said that the true purpose of education is to learn how to learn. That doesn't mean to learn how to jump through hoops at someone else's command. It doesn't mean doing assignments that someone else told you to do. It means finding out how to access and apply information, to develop and build perspectives, to learn how to challenge the assumptions that are holding you back. You might learn some of those skills in an Ivy League college, but you'll have a much easier time learning them elsewhere.

An Ivy League degree is like a Rolex watch. It's sort of prestigious, and totally unnecessary. It may help someone give you the initial benefit of the doubt, but if the substance of your mind and character doesn't match up, it won't make any difference. And just as you don't need a Rolex to be exceptional, you don't need any degree to be exceptional.

Despite their current but fading prestige, Ivy League colleges are essentially socialist backwaters that teach entitlement and alcoholism. Ability, perseverance, responsibility, and creativity matter far more than any degree they can give you.

I hope this book helps you manipulate the weak-minded, socialist drunkards that work at the admissions offices of American universities, in order to serve your own personal self-interest. If you have any questions, or if you want to learn more about what we do at Vohra Method, visit us at **VohraMethod.com.**

ABOUT ARVIN VOHRA:

Described as America's most ruthless college strategist, Arvin Vohra has helped students from all over the country get into top tier Ivy League colleges. In How to Get into an Ivy League College, he describes the clean and dirty tricks his students have used to get an unfair advantage over their competitors.

He is also the author of Lies, Damned Lies, and College Admissions, and The Equation for Excellence: How to Make Your Child Excel at Math.